METAVERSE
CANVAS

EDUARD ROSICART

ISBN: 9798851392320

For my parents, who have always been a source of inspiration and have pushed me towards non-conformism. Their faith in me has been the fuel and motivation to never give up.

CONTENTS

INTRODUCTION

In the introduction to this book, I would like to take you through a very personal journey. My name is Eduard Rosicart, and I have been working as an entrepreneur for most of my adult life. Over the years, I have immersed myself in various industries, built companies from scratch, and experienced both the successes and failures that any entrepreneur could expect. However, throughout all this time, I have always maintained a common thread: my insatiable desire to learn and to understand what comes after learning.

In recent years, that concern has led me to an emerging phenomenon that I consider to be the next frontier in technology and business: the metaverse. From the moment I had my first encounter with this concept, I knew something big was about to happen. I understood that we were on the verge of a new era of technological disruption, one that would change the way we live, work and play. But I also understood that while the way we interacted with technology was changing, the fundamentals of business remained constant.

In fact, throughout my career, I have relied on tools such as the *Business Model Canvas* and *Lean Canvas* to structure and shape my ideas. These tools have allowed me to understand

and break down the complexities of the business world, giving me the clarity I needed to take my ideas from concept to reality.

So when I started exploring the metaverse, I knew I needed a similar tool. I needed something that would allow me to navigate this new terrain, that would provide me with a framework for understanding how business is created in this new environment. Thus was born the **Metaverse Canvas**, a tool designed to help us explore and understand the business world in the metaverse.

Therefore, this book is the result of all that. It is the culmination of my experience as an entrepreneur, my passion for technology and my desire to understand what's next. But, more than anything else, this book is an invitation. An invitation to join me on this journey through the metaverse, to explore its infinite possibilities and to discover together how we can leverage its potential in our own businesses.

I hope you find it as fascinating and stimulating as I do.

1

THE RISE OF THE METAVERSE AND ITS IMPACT ON BUSINESS

The metaverse is a shared and persistent virtual environment where users can interact, socialize, create and trade in real time. In recent years, the metaverse has experienced exponential growth, driven by the massive adoption of emerging technologies such as virtual reality (VR), augmented reality (AR) and artificial intelligence (AI).

The metaverse is transforming the way we do business by offering new market opportunities and challenges for companies of all sizes and sectors. Businesses in the metaverse can tap into a global audience, deliver immersive and personalized experiences, and generate revenue by selling digital goods and services. In addition, the metaverse enables companies to establish closer relationships with their customers and partners, as well as to foster innovation and collaboration between teams and organizations.

1.1. The importance of digital marketing and strategic direction in the metaverse.

Digital marketing is essential to the success of any business in the metaverse, as it allows companies to reach their target audience, build and maintain a strong online presence, and optimize their marketing and sales efforts. Digital marketing in the metaverse encompasses a wide range of tactics and channels, such as online advertising, social media marketing, content marketing, email marketing, SEO and affiliate marketing, among others.

Strategic management, on the other hand, is the process of planning, implementing and evaluating a company's actions and resources to achieve its long-term objectives. In the context of the metaverse, strategic management involves identifying business opportunities, designing and adapting business models, establishing partnerships and collaborations, and measuring and adjusting performance and results.

1.2. The Metaverse Canvas: a tool for business modeling in the metaverse

The metaverse, as a new digital horizon, poses unprecedented challenges and opportunities that require adapted tools for their understanding and exploitation. In this context, the Metaverse Canvas emerges, a tool that, just as the Business Model Canvas did for digital business, is proposed as the reference framework for the design and evaluation of business models in the metaverse.

The Metaverse Canvas is an innovative, practical and adaptable guide that seeks to address the complexity of the metaverse and turn it into a series of manageable components. Its design is inspired by the Lean Canvas and the Business Model Canvas, but is adapted and expanded to capture the peculiarities of the metaverse. It consists of ten key elements: solution, target audience, channels, immersive experience, revenue streams, key metrics, NFT, competitive advantage, key alliances and cost structure. Each of these elements provides a piece of the puzzle that is a business model in the metaverse.

The relevance of the Metaverse Canvas lies in its ability to provide a logical and coherent structure that allows professionals and students of the digital environment to approach the design of a business model in the metaverse in a systematic and effective way. By breaking down the business model into these ten components, the Metaverse Canvas allows users to focus on each aspect of their business model individually, while maintaining an overall view of how each component interacts with the rest.

In addition, the Metaverse Canvas provides a valuable solution for professionals and students seeking to understand, innovate and succeed in the metaverse. It offers a common language that facilitates communication and understanding of complex ideas, and a visual format that helps visualize the business model in a clear and understandable way. In addition, its flexibility makes it adaptable to a wide range of businesses and sectors, allowing each user to customize it according to their specific needs.

1.2.1. The Metaverse Canvas and the development of products, services or applications in the metaverse

The development of products, services or applications in the metaverse represents a complex and challenging task. Unlike traditional digital environments, the metaverse is characterized by its immensity, interactivity and immersiveness, which requires novel approaches to the design and implementation of digital solutions in it.

The Metaverse Canvas is presented as a fundamental tool in this context, as it provides a framework for the analysis, design and implementation of digital solutions in the metaverse. By breaking down the business model into its ten fundamental components, the Metaverse Canvas enables practitioners and developers to understand and address each aspect of their solution individually and consistently.

In the development of a product, service or application, the Metaverse Canvas facilitates the identification and definition of key aspects such as the target audience, delivery channels, immersive experience, revenue sources and strategic alliances. At the same time, it allows to evaluate the feasibility and potential of the proposed solution, identifying associated costs and key metrics for performance monitoring.

In addition, the Metaverse Canvas offers a structured approach to innovation in the metaverse. By providing a global view of how each component of the business model interacts with the others, the Metaverse Canvas encourages the identification of opportunities for innovation and improvement in each area of the business model.

1.2.2. The Metaverse Canvas and digital marketing strategies in the Metaverse

The metaverse is not only a space for the development and implementation of products, services or applications, but also a rich and diverse environment for the execution of digital marketing strategies. As in product development, the Metaverse Canvas plays a crucial role in the planning and execution of these strategies.

Digital marketing in the metaverse differs significantly from traditional digital marketing strategies. The immersiveness and interactivity of the metaverse requires a more participatory and experiential approach, and the Metaverse Canvas can help marketers adapt to these new needs.

Using the Metaverse Canvas, marketers can clearly identify and define their target audience in the metaverse, design immersive experiences that attract and retain these users, and select the most effective channels to deliver those experiences. In addition, the Metaverse Canvas provides a framework for defining key revenue streams and partnerships that can support and enhance marketing strategies.

In addition, the inclusion of NFTs and competitive advantages in the Metaverse Canvas allows marketers to explore new ways to engage and monetize, and differentiate their offerings in the competitive metaverse environment.

Finally, the Metaverse Canvas includes a focus on key metrics and cost structure, ensuring that digital marketing strategies in the metaverse are measurable, cost-effective and results-driven.

2

THE METAVERSE CANVAS AND ITS TEN COMPONENTS

2.1. Solution: Creating value in the Metaverse

Value creation is the fundamental pillar of any business, and, in the metaverse environment, this is no exception. However, the metaverse, with its immersive and interactive experience, already provides a wide range of opportunities to create value in innovative and meaningful ways. The solution you offer in this environment, whether it is a product, service, experience or marketing campaign, is the vehicle through which you can deliver that value to your target audience.

In this context, the solution in the metaverse must be designed to meet the needs and desires of your target audience, and it must be unique and well differentiated to stand out in an increasingly competitive digital space. Most importantly, it must offer tangible and perceivable value that motivates your target audience to interact with it and, eventually, to become loyal customers.

2.1.1. Defining the Value Proposition

A value proposition is a clear statement that explains how the product, service or experience you offer solves problems, satisfies needs or improves the situation of your target audience. In the context of the metaverse, the value proposition acquires an additional dimension, since we are not only talking about goods or services in the traditional sense, but also about immersive experiences and interaction possibilities that transcend the limits of physical reality.

Defining an effective value proposition is a critical step in developing your business model in the metaverse. This not only helps guide the design and development of your offerings, but also provides a framework on which to focus your marketing and sales efforts. With a well-defined value proposition, you can effectively communicate what you do, who you do it for and why you do it, in a way that others cannot.

In the metaverse, the value proposition can take many forms. It can be a unique gaming experience, an e-commerce platform with special features, a virtual space for collaboration and creativity, or anything else that satisfies a user need or desire.

When defining your value proposition, it is important to take into account the unique characteristics of the metaverse. For example, immersion, interactivity and customizability are key aspects that can help you stand out from the competition. Moreover, since the metaverse is a digital space, the possibilities for innovation and experimentation are almost endless.

2.1.2. Value Proposition in Metaverse Products and Services

In the metaverse, products and services are not limited to standard physical or digital goods. They can range from immersive, personalized experiences to unique opportunities for interaction and collaboration. The value proposition in this context focuses on how these products or services can improve users' lives by providing them with innovative and exciting solutions that go beyond what traditional channels offer.

When it comes to products and services in the metaverse, the value proposition can be very diverse. For example, a video game company can offer a unique gaming experience in which players can fully immerse themselves in a virtual world, interact with other players in a meaningful way, and customize the game experience to their liking.

On the other hand, an e-commerce retailer can offer an immersive online shopping experience that allows customers to virtually "walk" through the store, "try on" clothing and accessories, and receive personalized recommendations based on their preferences and purchase history.

Another example might be a training company offering learning programs in the metaverse, providing students with an immersive and collaborative learning experience, which is not possible in traditional learning environments.

In all these cases, the value proposition lies in the way the product or service uses the features and possibilities of the metaverse to offer a unique and attractive solution to users' problems or needs.

In this regard, it is important to remember that the value proposition must be user-centric. It's not just about what your product or service can do, but how it can improve the lives of your users. Therefore, when developing your value proposition, it is essential that you put yourself in your users' shoes and consider their needs, wants and expectations.

2.1.3. Value Proposition in Metaverse Marketing Campaigns

The metaverse, being an immersive and participatory digital space, offers endless possibilities for marketing campaigns. In this context, the value proposition should not only be based on the tangible benefits of a product or service, but also on the memorable and exciting experiences that brands can create for their audiences.

In metaverse marketing campaigns, the value proposition can be the opportunity to participate in a unique experience that reinforces the emotional bond with the brand. This can involve immersive and personalized interactions with products, exclusive virtual events, or even the opportunity to be part of a virtual community built around the brand.

For example, a fashion brand may launch an exclusive clothing collection in the metaverse, allowing users to "try on" and purchase the items in a virtual environment, before making the purchase in the real world. This not only offers a new way to interact with products, but also creates a unique and exciting shopping experience that can strengthen the customer's relationship with the brand.

Another example might be a beverage brand hosting an exclusive virtual concert in the metaverse, where fans can interact with the music and other attendees in a way that would not be possible at a traditional concert.

These experiences, made possible by the interactivity and immersion of the metaverse, can become a powerful value proposition for marketing campaigns, helping brands stand out in an increasingly saturated marketplace, and build stronger, more meaningful relationships with their audiences.

2.1.4. Web3 and the New Possibilities of Value Creation

Web3, also known as the semantic web, marks the next evolutionary step in the history of the Internet. Unlike Web2, which was centralized and controlled by large corporations, Web3 is a vision of a decentralized, blockchain-based web that returns control and ownership of data to users. This paradigm shift opens up new possibilities for value creation in the metaverse.

On the Web3, users can own and control unique digital assets, known as non-fungible tokens (NTFs). These can represent anything from digital art and music, to virtual terrains and avatars in the metaverse. This allows brands to create new forms of value, such as unique digital products that can be bought, sold and collected.

In addition, Web3 allows brands and users to interact on a deeper and more meaningful level. Users can participate directly in brand communities, contributing ideas and feedback, and can be rewarded for their participation with tokens. This creates a positive feedback loop that can strengthen the relationship between brands and their communities.

Finally, the decentralization of Web3 also opens up new opportunities for cooperation and collaboration. Instead of competing in a zero-sum marketplace, brands can work together to create richer, more valuable user experiences. For example, they could collaborate in the development of shared virtual spaces, or in the creation of interactive user experiences that combine different products and services.

2.1.5. Engaging the Audience in the Metaverse

In today's digital environment, audience participation is not only desirable, but essential. In the metaverse, this premise is elevated to a new level. Here, experiences are more immersive, interactive and personalized, offering brands new and exciting ways to engage their audiences.

The key to effective participation in the metaverse is to understand that it is not just about promoting a product or service, but about fostering unique experiences and communities. Metaverse users are looking for meaningful and authentic interactions, not just advertising. Brands that can deliver these experiences will benefit from increased engagement, loyalty and, ultimately, success in their efforts.

In the metaverse, brands have the opportunity to interact with their audience in ways that go beyond the possibilities of Web2. Immersive experiences, such as live events, meetings and gaming experiences, can help create a deeper connection between the brand and its audience. In addition, brands can use blockchain technology to offer exclusive rewards and benefits to their most engaged followers, such as access to exclusive content or the ability to own a piece of the brand in the form of tokens.

In addition, by leveraging the interactivity of the metaverse, brands can encourage active participation from their audience. For example, they can invite users to contribute their ideas and opinions, participate in challenges and competitions, or collaborate in the creation of new experiences and products.

2.2. Target audience

In the vast and diversified world of the metaverse, the correct identification of the target audience is critical to the success of any value proposition. Without a precise and prior knowledge of who we are targeting, the risk of developing solutions that are disconnected from the needs and expectations of users is high.

The metaverse, with its wide range of experiences and applications, welcomes a heterogeneous audience, whose interests, motivations and behaviors vary significantly. In this scenario, target segmentation is not only a strategic activity, but a basic requirement.

Identifying the target audience in the metaverse requires a multidimensional approach, encompassing demographic, geographic, psychographic, and behavioral factors, with a special emphasis on preferences and expectations related to immersive and digital experiences. In addition, the diversity of platforms and technologies available in the metaverse demands a deep understanding of how and where our target audience interacts in this digital space.

Once you have a clear idea of your solution, the next step is to identify who it is aimed at. Your target audience are the people who will benefit most from your solution and are therefore most likely to become your customers.

To identify your target audience, you need to think about who these people are, how they behave in the metaverse and what they are looking for. Here are some questions to help you do that:

- How old are they?
- What metaverse platforms do you use?
- How do they spend their time in the metaverse?
- What kind of content or experiences are they looking for?
- How could your solution improve their experience in the metaverse?

The more you know about your target audience, the better you can design your product or service to meet their needs and desires. And, once you know who you are targeting, you will also be able to make more informed decisions about how and where to promote your offer in the metaverse.

2.2.1. Target Audience Analysis and Segmentation

Target audience segmentation is an essential task, which allows us to precisely target the value propositions of our business. Target audience analysis involves a detailed assessment of the various groups of people who might be interested in our products or services. This analysis should address both the demographics and psychographics of that audience, including age, gender, income level, location, interests, attitudes and behavior.

Segmentation, on the other hand, involves dividing the target audience into smaller, more manageable groups, according to their common characteristics. These segments can be as broad or as narrow as necessary, and can be based on any criteria that are relevant to our business. Examples of segmentation criteria could include affinity with technology, interest in the metaverse, level of engagement in existing metaverse platforms, among others.

Once we have identified and segmented our target audience, it is important to maintain an up-to-date understanding of their motivations, preferences and expectations. In the metaverse, where trends and technologies change rapidly, keeping up with the changing needs and desires of our target audience is essential to adapt our marketing solution and strategy effectively. In the following subchapters, we will explore the different types of audiences that may be interested in the metaverse, depending on their generation and the different platforms they use.

2.2.2. Generations and their relationship with the Metaverse

Each generation has distinctive and unique characteristics, and their relationship with technology and, more specifically, with the metaverse, also varies significantly. Therefore, it is essential to understand these generational differences in order to plan business and marketing strategies in the metaverse.

Starting with the Baby Boomers, although they are generally considered less tech-savvy than younger generations, they should not be overlooked. Many have actively embraced the technology and may be interested in exploring the opportunities that the metaverse can offer them, especially in terms of social interaction and cultural experiences.

Generation X, often described as the bridge generation between digital natives and non-natives, has proven to be adaptable to new technologies. Your relationship with the metaverse can be varied, from use for entertainment to commerce to training and professional development.

Millennials, digital natives, have grown up with technology and are quick to adapt to new platforms. They are highly adept at social networking and digital consumption, which can translate to an interest in immersive metaverse experiences.

Generation Z, the youngest and most technologically fluent generation, has proven to be incredibly adaptable to new platforms and forms of digital interaction. Their familiarity with online gaming and virtual reality platforms may lead to faster and deeper adoption of the metaverse.

It is important to note that, although these generations have distinctive characteristics, the dividing lines are not absolute and there may be considerable overlap and individual variability. However, understanding these generational trends can help companies better address their target audience and adapt their business and marketing strategies in the metaverse.

2.2.3. Different Audience Types According to Metaverse Platforms

The diversity of platforms within the metaverse in turn reflects the diversity of target audiences. Each platform has a unique approach and appeal, and appeals to a particular type of user.

Gaming platforms, such as Roblox and Fortnite, appeal to a younger audience, who enjoy social interaction and competitive play. These platforms have proven particularly effective in appealing to Generation Z and Millennials, who are accustomed to the immersive and social experiences these games offer.

Virtual reality platforms, such as Oculus and HTC Vive, appeal to an audience looking for a more immersive and realistic experience. This audience tends to be more technologically advanced and is willing to invest in specialized hardware to access these experiences.

E-commerce and social commerce platforms in the metaverse, such as Decentraland and Somnium Space, attract an audience interested in virtual property and commercial transactions. This audience can include investors and entrepreneurs, as well as artists and creators, who are looking for new ways to monetize their work.

Networking and collaboration platforms in the metaverse, such as Spatial and VirBELA, appeal to a more professional audience looking to improve collaboration and productivity in a virtual environment. This audience can include professionals from all fields and sectors, from education and training to consulting and software development.

It is crucial for companies and marketers to understand these differences and select the platforms that best align with their target audience and business objectives. In addition, they should keep an eye on trends and changes in the metaverse landscape, as new platforms and opportunities can quickly emerge in this dynamic and constantly evolving space.

2.2.4. Audience Expectations and Motivations in the Metaverse

Understanding the expectations and motivations of the target audience is essential to designing products, services or marketing campaigns that are effective in the metaverse. Motivations for participating in the metaverse are diverse and can range from a desire to explore new and exciting worlds, to interest in social interaction, learning, entertainment, content creation and virtual commerce, among others.

1. **Exploration and Adventure**: The ability to discover and explore immersive and detailed virtual worlds is a powerful motivation for many metaverse users. The desire to experience the unknown, to travel to places unreachable in the physical world, and to experience extraordinary adventures can be a great attraction.

2. **Social Interaction**: The metaverse offers new and exciting forms of social interaction. Users can communicate and collaborate with others in real time, regardless of their geographic location. This can be particularly attractive to younger generations, who value opportunities for socialization and community.

3. **Learning and Development**: The metaverse also offers unique opportunities for learning and personal and professional development. Total immersion experiences can facilitate understanding and retention of information, and can be especially effective for training and education.

4. **Entertainment and Gaming**: Games and entertainment experiences are a big part of the appeal of the metaverse. From competitive games to immersive narrative experiences, the metaverse can offer a wide range of entertainment experiences.

5. **Creation and Expression**: The metaverse is a blank canvas for creativity and expression. Users can create and customize their own content, from avatars and virtual objects to landscapes and entire worlds.

6. **Trade and Business**: Last but not least, the metaverse also offers opportunities for trade and business. Users can buy, sell and trade virtual goods and services, and companies can leverage the metaverse as a new sales and marketing channel.

Understanding these motivations and aligning them with the value proposition of your product, service or marketing campaign in the metaverse is essential to attract and retain your target audience.

2.2.5. Adaptation of the Solution and Marketing Strategy to the Target Audience

The key to achieving an effective and meaningful presence in the metaverse lies in the ability to adapt your marketing solution and strategy to the needs, expectations and motivations of your target audience. This adaptation must be done at different levels:

1. **Solution Adjustment**: Depending on your target audience, the solution you offer in the metaverse can vary greatly. If your audience is predominantly young and interested in gaming and socializing, an entertainment or social interaction oriented solution might be the best fit. On the other hand, if your target audience is more

interested in learning and development, a solution that offers immersive educational experiences could be the most effective in this case.

2. **Personalization of the Experience**: The metaverse allows a high degree of customization, which is an advantage when it comes to meeting the specific needs of different segments of the target audience. From customizing avatars and environments, to tailoring the interface and functionality according to user preferences and skills, personalization can significantly improve the user experience and increase user engagement and satisfaction.

3. **Marketing and Communication Strategy**: Your marketing and communication strategy must also be tailored to your target audience. This includes choosing the most effective communication channels, developing messages that identify with your audience's motivations and values, and creating marketing campaigns that are engaging and relevant to them.

4. **Feedback and Continuous Improvement**: It is important to remember that adapting to your target audience is an ongoing process. As you learn more about your audience and receive their feedback on your solution and marketing strategy, you should be willing to make adjustments and improvements. This will not only allow you to maintain the relevance and attractiveness of your offering, but will also help you maintain a competitive

edge in the dynamic and rapidly changing environment of the metaverse.

Ultimately, tailoring the solution and marketing strategy to the target audience is critical to success in the metaverse. By doing so, you will not only improve your audience satisfaction and engagement, but you will also increase the effectiveness and return on your investment in the metaverse.

2.3. Channels

Channels represent the bridge that links our value proposition with our target audience in the metaverse. Identifying and selecting the right channels, whether metaverse platforms or other digital marketing channels, is a crucial aspect for the successful implementation of any metaverse strategy.

In the metaverse, as in any digital environment, channels are the routes through which users interact with brands and experience their products or services. They can be specialized platforms, such as Spatial, Decentraland, Roblox, or they can be various digital marketing strategies that allow us to capture, attract and retain our audience.

The selection of the right channels must be aligned with our value proposition, and be precisely targeted to our target audience. Not all channels will be suitable for all brands, products, services or experiences. Some will be more effective for certain types of audiences, objectives or value propositions. Therefore, we must deeply understand the characteristics, advantages and limitations of each channel, and how these can be used to enhance our value proposition and achieve our strategic objectives in the metaverse.

In the following subsections, we will dive into channel choice and management, examine the differences between digital marketing channels and metaverse platforms, and provide clear examples of their effective use. In this way, we will propose a complete framework that will allow the most appropriate selection and efficient management of channels in the metaverse.

Connecting with the public in the metaverse

Channels are the vital artery that connects companies with their target audience in the metaverse. They are the channel through which communication, distribution and solution sales flow, and are therefore crucial to the scope and effectiveness of marketing strategies and customer satisfaction.

In the metaverse, the concept of channel acquires an additional dimension. It is not only about traditional digital media such as websites, mobile applications or social networks. In the metaverse, the platforms themselves, such as Spatial, Decentraland, Roblox, among others, become channels in themselves, offering immersive experiences to users and enabling deep and meaningful interactions.

This dualism in the nature of channels in the metaverse makes them a key element in defining the value proposition and marketing strategy. On the one hand, we have traditional digital marketing channels that allow us to engage and direct audiences to our products and services in the metaverse. On the other hand, the metaverse platforms become channels to interact directly with the public in an immersive and digital environment.

2.3.1. Digital Marketing Channels for Audience Engagement

In the digital age, audience engagement is a crucial factor for any business. Digital marketing channels are fundamental tools to attract, inform and persuade potential customers. In the context of the metaverse, these channels can be used to direct the audience to the immersive experiences on offer.

Digital marketing channels include a variety of platforms and methods, such as social media, search engines, email, online ads and content marketing. Each of these channels has its own characteristics and advantages, so it is essential to select the most appropriate ones to reach your target audience.

- **Social Networking**: Social networks such as Facebook, Instagram, Twitter, LinkedIn and TikTok are critical for audience engagement. With millions of daily active users, they allow brands to interact directly with their target audience, promote their products and services in the metaverse and drive traffic to their platforms.

- **Search engines**: Google, Bing and other search engines are essential for audience acquisition. Through search engine optimization (SEO) and search engine advertising

(SEM), companies can increase their online visibility and attract more users to their platforms in the metaverse.

- **E-mail**: Email continues to be an effective digital marketing channel. Through newsletters and personalized email campaigns, companies can keep their target audience informed about the latest news and experiences in the metaverse.

- **Online ads**: Online ads on platforms such as Google AdWords, Facebook Ads and others allow businesses to reach a wider audience and drive traffic to their metaverse platforms.

- **Content marketing**: Creating and sharing relevant and valuable content is an excellent way to attract and retain an audience. This can include blogs, videos, podcasts, infographics, among others, that inform and excite the audience about experiences in the metaverse.

When selecting your channels, you should consider not only where your target audience is located, but also which channels best align with your solution. For example, if your solution is a new type of interactive content, a game or a virtual world may be the most appropriate channel. If your solution involves the sale of digital goods, an NFT platform might be the most appropriate channel.

Defining **user acquisition channels** is crucial in any digital marketing strategy, and the metaverse is no exception. Below, we provide a list of the main user acquisition channels for different generations and the reason for their effectiveness:

- **Generation Z (born between 1997 and 2012)**: Social networks such as Instagram, TikTok and Snapchat are extremely popular among this group. In addition, video game platforms such as Fortnite and Roblox are also a great way to engage Generation Z users. These platforms allow for more direct and creative interaction, which makes them especially attractive to this age group.

- **Millennials (born between 1981 and 1996)**: Facebook, YouTube and Twitter are the most effective channels to reach millennials. In addition, streaming platforms such as Twitch and Netflix are also very popular. Millennials value quality content and social interaction, so these channels are ideal for capturing their attention.

- **Generation X (born between 1965 and 1980)**: This generation still uses more traditional channels, such as email and search engines. However, they are also present in social networks such as Facebook and LinkedIn. Likewise, news platforms and blogs can also be effective in reaching this group.

- **Baby Boomers (born between 1946 and 1964)**: Boomers tend to prefer more traditional channels such as email, search engines and online newspapers. However, they are also increasingly present in social networks such as Facebook. Online television and digital radio platforms can also be effective channels for engaging users of this generation.

Example 1: Fornite

One of the most illustrative cases of the effective use of digital marketing channels for audience engagement is Epic Games' deployment of strategies to promote its popular video game Fortnite.

Fortnite is not just a video game, it has become a social and cultural space, a virtual meeting place for millions of players around the world. To keep its audience hooked and attract new players, Epic Games has organized virtual in-game events, most notably the virtual concert "Travis Scott: Astronomical".

To promote this event, Epic Games used a combination of digital marketing channels. First, they announced the event through their own social networks and those of artist Travis Scott, creating excitement among their followers. In addition, they used blog posts and video game-related websites to reach a wider audience.

On the other hand, they conducted a mass emailing to registered Fortnite users, informing them about the event and motivating them to participate. They also took advantage of online advertising, buying advertising space on platforms such as Google AdWords and Facebook Ads.

As a result of this multi-channel strategy, the event "Travis Scott: Astronomical" was a resounding success, attracting more than 27 million players during its run, setting a new record for Fortnite and demonstrating the power of digital marketing channels for audience engagement in the metaverse.

Example 2: Decentraland

Another notable case of effective use of digital marketing channels for audience engagement is the launch of the "Decentraland MANA" cryptocurrency.

Decentraland is a decentralized virtual world in which users can own parcels of virtual land, create and monetize content, and interact with other users. The launch of its proprietary cryptocurrency, MANA, was crucial to its development and growth.

To promote the launch of MANA, Decentraland used various digital marketing channels. First, it partnered with influencers and content creators in the cryptocurrency space to generate interest and brand recognition. These influencers shared information about MANA and Decentraland on their respective social media platforms, blogs and podcasts, reaching millions of followers interested in cryptocurrencies and blockchain technology.

In addition, Decentraland used online advertising platforms such as Google AdWords and Facebook Ads to promote its launch. Through these platforms, they reached a specific global audience interested in cryptocurrencies and virtual worlds.

Finally, they conducted a series of airdrops, or free cryptocurrency distributions, to attract new users to their platform. These airdrops were advertised through their own social media and communication channels, as well as through the channels of affiliated influencers.

As a result of this multi-channel digital marketing strategy, MANA's launch was a success, attracting millions of new users to Decentraland and establishing MANA as one of the leading cryptocurrencies in the metaverse space.

2.3.2. Metaverse Platforms as Channels

Metaverse platforms offer a unique immersive space for companies to interact with their target audience. These platforms are emerging channels, as they combine technologies such as virtual reality, augmented reality and artificial intelligence to provide immersive and personalized experiences that are unique to each user. This type of interaction is becoming increasingly relevant as audiences demand more personalized and immersive experiences.

These platforms are becoming powerful channels for companies for several reasons. First, companies can create immersive experiences that reinforce their brand and connect with their audience in new and exciting ways. Secondly, these platforms allow companies to interact with their audience in a more direct and personalized way. Third, metaverse platforms also offer unique opportunities for collaboration and co-creation with users.

A crucial aspect to keep in mind is that these platforms are usually decentralized, meaning that they are not controlled by a single entity, but are owned by the community of users that inhabit them. This poses unique challenges and opportunities, such as the need to adopt community engagement and collaboration strategies.

Choosing the right metaverse platform as a channel depends on the target audience, business objectives and company capabilities. Therefore, it is crucial to understand the metaverse ecosystem, as well as the features and advantages of each platform, before making a decision.

Here we share a list of some of the major platforms in the metaverse along with their target audience and the type of business objectives that may be appropriate for each:

1. **Roblox**: It is a gaming and game creation platform that has captured the Z generation and younger users. Its audience is mainly composed of children under 16 years of age. This platform would be ideal for brands looking to target this demographic, such as toy, education or entertainment companies.

2. **Fortnite**: This multiplayer online game is popular among generation Z and millennials. It hosts virtual events, concerts and product launches, making it ideal for brands looking to generate awareness and excitement around a new product or event.

3. **Decentraland**: It is a blockchain-powered virtual reality platform where users own and control the virtual land and assets. Its audience is diverse, but includes cryptocurrency and virtual reality enthusiasts. Companies looking to explore trading virtual goods or hosting virtual events may want to consider this platform.

4. **Spatial**: This virtual reality collaboration platform is popular in the business world. It is ideal for companies looking to facilitate virtual meetings, conferences or training. Its target audience would include professionals and companies.

5. **VRChat**: It is a virtual reality social platform that allows users to interact in three-dimensional environments. It has a diverse audience, but is popular among virtual reality users and gamers. This platform could be suitable for companies looking to encourage social interaction with their brand.

Brands should choose the platform that most closely aligns with their target audience and business objectives. In addition, they should consider the type of experience they can offer on each platform and how it can enhance the relationship with their audience.

Example 1: Travis Scott and his concert to promote Fornite

A prime example of the effective use of a metaverse platform as a channel is Travis Scott's virtual concert in Fortnite. This event, called "Astronomical", was held in April 2020 and broke records, with more than 12.3 million players participating in the live concert.

Epic Games, the company behind Fortnite, and Travis Scott worked together to create a ten-minute show that combined music with stunning visual effects. Players were able to experience the concert in first person, interacting with the environment and seeing Scott in different shapes and sizes during the performance.

In addition to the concert itself, Epic Games also released a number of Travis Scott merchandise in the game, such as skins, emotes and more, which generated additional engagement and sales. In addition, Travis Scott themed missions were added for players to complete, further encouraging interaction with the event.

The Travis Scott concert is an excellent example of how brands can use metaverse platforms as effective channels. Epic Games and Scott not only managed to attract a large audience, but also created an interactive and immersive experience that succeeded with Fortnite's player base. Through this unique experience, Scott was able to promote his music to a global audience and Epic Games was able to increase engagement on its platform, demonstrating the potential of the metaverse for promotion and content marketing.

Example 2: Tesla and its Cyber Truck in Roblox

Another outstanding case of the use of the metaverse as a channel is the presentation of the Tesla Cyber Truck in Roblox. Roblox, being a metaverse platform popular among young users, offers a digital space where players can interact with environments and objects in a game format.

Tesla took advantage of this platform to present its new car model, the Cyber Truck, at an interactive event. Players had the opportunity to see the vehicle up close and experience a driving simulation, providing a unique and exciting experience that went beyond a conventional product presentation. This allowed Tesla to reach a young and highly engaged audience, creating excitement and curiosity around its new product.

In addition, the event offered players the opportunity to "buy" the Cyber Truck in the game, encouraging interaction and participation. This level of interactivity and the opportunity to experience the product first-hand created a lasting impression on gamers, boosting Tesla's visibility and impact in this demographic market.

This example illustrates how brands can use metaverse platforms to present products in an innovative and engaging way. Rather than limiting itself to traditional marketing channels, Tesla used Roblox to create an immersive and memorable experience that would capture the attention of a strategic target audience. In doing so, he demonstrated the potential of the metaverse to innovate the way brands interact and connect with their audiences.

2.3.3. Channel Selection and Management in the Metaverse

The choice and management of channels in the metaverse are essential factors for the success of any business or marketing strategy in this space. As in the physical world, selecting the right channels allows you to reach your target audience effectively, while effective management ensures brand consistency and optimization of resources.

First, the choice of channels in the metaverse must be based on a clear understanding of the target audience. As we have discussed in previous sections, different generations and types of audiences may have different preferences in terms of metaverse platforms. Therefore, it is crucial to select the channels that best align with the expectations and behaviors of our target audience.

In addition, the choice of channels must take into account the type of product or service being offered, as well as the objectives of the marketing campaign. For example, if the goal is to increase brand awareness among a young audience, it may be beneficial to use a metaverse platform popular with that demographic, such as Roblox. On the other hand, if you offer a high-end product or service, it may be more appropriate to choose a platform that has a perception of quality and exclusivity.

Once the channels have been selected, it is essential to manage them effectively. This involves maintaining an active and consistent presence, adapting content and interactions to the particularities of each channel and monitoring performance, so that adjustments can be made when necessary. Effective channel management also includes managing security and privacy, which is especially important in the metaverse because of the implications of Web3 and digital property.

Finally, it is important to remember that the choice and management of channels in the metaverse is not a single decision, but an ongoing process. As metaverse platforms evolve and audience behaviors change, companies must be willing to adapt their channel strategy to remain relevant and effective.

2.4. Immersive experience

In the increasingly digital context in which we live, differentiation and the ability to generate value for the customer are crucial factors for the success of any business. In this sense, the immersive experience is presented as an innovative and differentiating element with respect to Web 2.0, which can mark a before and after in the relationship with the customer and in marketing strategies.

The immersive experience is based on the creation of virtual environments and situations in which users are not mere spectators, but active participants. It's about making them feel that they are part of the experience, that they are really present and involved in the action. This can increase customer engagement and satisfaction, improve brand recall and brand image, and generate a positive emotional impact that motivates users to act.

The immersive experience can be a central element in the value proposition of a business in the metaverse. It can help create a deeper and more meaningful connection with the customer, more effectively convey brand values and purpose, and provide added value that makes products or services stand out in the marketplace.

Likewise, the immersive experience can be a powerful tool in metaverse marketing strategies. It can enable brands to tell more immersive and persuasive stories, create more interactive and personalized campaigns, and provide unique experiences that generate awareness and conversations around the brand.

However, to design effective immersive experiences, factors such as content quality, interactivity and personalization, accessibility and usability, and the integration of emerging technologies such as VR, AR, MR and XR need to be taken into account.

In the following sections, we will delve deeper into these aspects and explore how immersive experiences can contribute to value creation in the metaverse.

2.4.1. The Immersive Experience as a Value Proposition and Brand Expression

The immersive experience is a powerful tool for creating unique and compelling value propositions that stand out in the metaverse. The ability to immerse the user in a completely new and immersive environment opens up an infinite range of possibilities to deliver value and express the essence of the brand.

A well-designed immersive experience can become an essential component of a brand's value proposition. By offering the user the opportunity to interact and actively participate in the metaverse environment, you can provide additional value beyond the simple product or service. It's about creating memorable and emotionally engaging moments that connect with the user on a deeper level.

In addition, immersive experiences are an excellent way to express brand identity and establish an emotional connection with the user. Through the careful choice of visual, audio and narrative elements of the immersive environment, the character, values and personality of the brand can be conveyed. Each interaction can be designed to reflect the brand's tone and reinforce its position in the user's mind.

At the same time, it is essential to keep in mind that immersive experiences must be designed with the user in mind. They should be accessible, easily navigable and offer meaningful and relevant interaction. Personalization can play an important role in this regard, and tailor the experience to the user's individual needs, preferences and expectations.

Therefore, the immersive experience becomes an essential component of the metaverse strategy, being both an integral part of the value proposition and a powerful tool to express the brand identity. In the following subsections, we will delve into the different forms of interaction possible in immersive environments, and how these can be used to enhance the value proposition and brand expression.

Case Study: The Gucci Immersive Experience on Roblox

An excellent example of how a brand has used the immersive experience to enhance its value proposition and express its identity is the campaign carried out by Gucci on the metaverse platform Roblox.

Gucci, the renowned luxury fashion brand, created the "Gucci Garden Experience" on Roblox, an immersive experience that allowed users to explore a virtual garden designed with the brand's aesthetics and values. This garden not only reflected Gucci's identity and creativity, but also offered a unique and personalized experience to each user. As users moved through the garden, their environment changed and adapted to their interaction, creating an experience of constant discovery and emotional connection with the brand.

In addition to the experience itself, Gucci also offered users the ability to purchase and wear virtual Gucci products within Roblox, adding an additional layer of interaction and personalization to the experience.

This Gucci campaign is a shining example of how a brand can use immersive experience to enhance its value proposition and strengthen its brand identity in the metaverse. Through this initiative, Gucci not only succeeded in connecting with a new generation of consumers in the metaverse, but also demonstrated how brands can transcend physical boundaries and create emotionally influential and highly personalized brand experiences in the virtual environment.

Case Study: Siemens Immersive Experience in Industry 4.0

A prominent example of how a company has used immersive experience in a B2B environment and in the industrial metaverse is Siemens and its Industry 4.0 concept.

Siemens, one of the giants in the technology and engineering industry, is using virtual reality (VR) and augmented reality (AR) to take the experience of its value proposition to another level. In its virtual pavilion "Digital Enterprise - Thinking industry further", Siemens presents its customers with a virtual tour of its vision of the industry of the future, providing an immersive experience in which visitors can explore the company's digital solutions interactively.

This digital pavilion offers a detailed tour of a digitized industrial plant, where visitors can see how the various Siemens components and solutions interact in a real industrial environment. Through this experience, Siemens not only demonstrates its competence and leadership in the digitalization and automation of industry, but also enables visitors to understand more concretely and tangibly the benefits and value that Siemens solutions can bring to their own operations.

This Siemens success story demonstrates how an immersive experience can be used effectively to enhance a company's value proposition in a B2B environment. By providing an interactive and highly visual experience, Siemens has been able to more effectively communicate the complexity and sophistication of its solutions, while strengthening its relationship with its customers by allowing them to experience firsthand the value Siemens can bring to their operations.

2.4.2. The Immersive Experience in Metaverse Marketing Strategies

In an increasingly digital world, the immersive experience has become a powerful tool for marketing strategies in the metaverse. The main objective of any marketing strategy is to capture the attention of the target audience and generate a lasting engagement with the brand. In this context, the immersive experience provides a unique opportunity to achieve these objectives in an innovative and effective way.

Marketing strategies in the metaverse can leverage the immersive experience to create more engaging and memorable advertising and promotional campaigns. By immersing users in an interactive virtual world, brands can generate a stronger emotional connection and higher brand retention compared to traditional marketing channels.

In addition, the immersive experience enables brands to provide personalized customer experiences. Machine learning algorithms can collect and analyze data on user behavior and preferences in the metaverse, allowing brands to adjust their marketing strategies and deliver personalized content that is tailored to each user's needs and desires.

However, to be effective, immersive marketing strategies must be carefully designed. Virtual environments must be easy to navigate and must offer a high quality user experience. In addition, brands must ensure that their immersive marketing strategies are ethical and respectful of user privacy.

In short, the immersive experience offers brands the opportunity to innovate their marketing strategies and connect with their target audience in new and exciting ways. However, to take full advantage of the opportunities offered by such an immersive experience, brands must combine a solid understanding of their target audience with a thoughtful, user-centric approach to good experience design.

2.4.3. Types of Interactions in Immersive Environments

The main appeal of immersive environments lies in their ability to provide rich and meaningful interactions that go beyond the possibilities of traditional media. These interactions not only allow users to interact with the virtual environment and its objects, but also facilitate communication and collaboration with other users. In this chapter, we will explore the types of interactions that can be generated in immersive environments of virtual reality (VR), augmented reality (AR), mixed reality (MR), and extended reality (XR).

1. **Interactions in Virtual Reality (VR)**: VR allows users to fully immerse themselves in a virtual environment, enabling highly immersive interactions. Users can explore the virtual environment, manipulate objects, and even interact with AI-controlled characters, or with other users in real time. Input devices, such as motion controllers and haptic devices, can further enhance immersion by allowing users to control their virtual actions intuitively and receive tactile feedback.

2. **Augmented Reality (AR) interactions**: AR overlays digital information onto the real world, allowing users to interact with virtual objects in their physical environment. Interactions in AR can be as simple as touching a virtual object on a mobile device screen, or as advanced as manipulating virtual objects in 3D space using motion tracking and gesture detection.

3. **Interactions in Mixed Reality (MR)**: MRI combines aspects of VR and AR to allow users to interact with virtual and physical objects in the same environment. In MRI, users can move freely and manipulate virtual objects as if they were real, providing an even greater level of interactivity and immersion.

4. **Interactions in Extended Reality (XR)**: XR is an umbrella term that encompasses all immersive technologies, including VR, AR, MRI and future technologies yet to be developed. Interactions in XR can vary widely, depending on the specific technology used, but all have the potential to offer immersive and highly interactive experiences.

In conclusion, each type of immersive environment offers unique opportunities for interaction, and the choice of technology depends on the goal of the experience. To design effective interactions in immersive environments, it is important to consider factors such as immersion, interactivity, usability and accessibility.

2.4.4. Virtual Reality (VR) in the Metaverse

Virtual Reality (VR) is a technology that is of key importance in the development of the metaverse, as it provides maximum immersion in a virtual environment completely generated by a computer. VR allows users to experience a sense of presence in the metaverse, interact with their environment in a natural way and feel truly "inside" the virtual world.

VR experiences in the metaverse can range from games and simulations to virtual tours and business meetings. In all cases, users interact with the virtual environment through input devices, such as VR goggles, motion controllers and other haptic devices, which enable interaction through gestures and body movements.

A very relevant application of VR in the metaverse is the sale of products or services. Companies can create virtual stores where users can examine products in 3D, interact with them and even "try them out" before buying. This type of interaction can improve the shopping experience and increase the conversion rate.

Another important use of VR in the metaverse is in marketing campaigns. Brands can create immersive experiences that engage users in a deeper and more personalized way than traditional media. For example, they can invite users to explore a themed virtual world, participate in a real-time virtual event, or interact with branded characters in a VR environment.

VR also has great potential for training and education in the metaverse. VR environments can provide a safe and controlled environment for technical and professional skills training, and can enhance learning by allowing students to explore concepts and phenomena in an interactive and visual way.

Finally, it is important to note that while VR offers maximum immersion, it can also present challenges in terms of accessibility and comfort. It is essential to take these factors into account when designing VR experiences in the metaverse to ensure a positive experience for all users.

2.4.5. Augmented Reality (AR) in the Metaverse

Augmented Reality (AR) is a technology that superimposes digital information, such as images, sounds and visual effects, on the real world, enriching our perception and providing a real-time interactive experience. Unlike virtual reality, AR does not require users to be fully immersed in a digital environment, allowing them greater flexibility and adaptability to various situations and contexts.

RA has several useful applications in the metaverse. In the field of product and service sales, for example, AR applications can be created that allow users to visualize products in their own environment, before making a purchase. This can be especially valuable for products such as furniture or clothing, where being able to see how the product fits into one's environment or body can significantly influence the purchase decision.

In terms of marketing strategies in the metaverse, AR can be used to create immersive experiences that pique users' curiosity and interest. For example, a brand could launch an AR scavenger hunt campaign that invites users to explore their city for digital rewards, or create custom AR filters that users can use and share on social media.

RA can also have a major impact on education and training in the metaverse. For example, AR applications can be developed for science education, allowing students to interact with 3D models of organisms and systems, providing a deeper and more visual understanding of concepts.

In the metaverse, AR can be a powerful way to combine the digital world with the physical world, creating unique and memorable experiences. However, as with VR, it is crucial to consider usability and accessibility when designing AR experiences, to ensure that these are engaging and accessible to all users.

2.4.6. Mixed Reality (MR) in the Metaverse

Mixed Reality (MR) is a technology that combines elements of Virtual Reality (VR) and Augmented Reality (AR). In an RM environment, users can interact with digital objects that are superimposed on the real world, creating a sense of immersion that goes beyond what VR and AR can offer separately.

In the context of the metaverse, RM can offer unique opportunities to create immersive and memorable experiences. For example, in the case of product or service sales, an RM application could allow users to interact with a digital product in their own environment, manipulate it and experiment with it as if it were real. This could be particularly useful for complex or customizable products, where direct interaction can provide a higher degree of understanding and satisfaction.

In terms of marketing strategies in the metaverse, RM can be used to create interactive campaigns that engage users and make them feel part of a unique experience. For example, an RM experience could be created that invites users to explore a virtual environment from their own home, discovering new products and offerings as they go.

In the field of training and education, RM can provide highly effective learning tools, allowing students to interact with study materials in a more practical and visual way.

It is important to note that, as with VR and AR, RM experience design must focus on accessibility and usability to ensure that all users can effectively participate. At the same time, it is critical to consider privacy and security issues, given the RM's ability to collect and process data about the user's environment and behavior.

2.4.7. Extended Reality (XR) in the Metaverse

Extended Reality (XR) is an umbrella term that encompasses all technologies that combine the physical and digital worlds, including Virtual Reality (VR), Augmented Reality (AR) and Mixed Reality (MR). The XR can provide a range of experiences, from total immersion in a fully digital environment, to overlaying digital elements in the real world.

In the metaverse, XR can be a very powerful tool for delivering immersive, personalized experiences that create value for both businesses and users. Depending on the context, it may be advantageous to use VR, AR, MR, or a combination of these technologies to create the most effective XR experience.

For selling products or services, the XR can allow users to visualize and customize products in a digital environment, test them in their own space, and even interact with them in a realistic way. This can provide a deeper understanding of the product, improve customer confidence, and increase the chances of conversion.

In marketing, XR can be used to create immersive, participatory campaigns that engage users and provide them with unique experiences. This can increase engagement, improve brand recall, and generate a positive emotional impact that motivates users to act.

Finally, it is important to keep in mind that while the XR offers tremendous opportunities, it also poses challenges in terms of accessibility, usability, privacy and security. Therefore, it is essential to address these aspects in the design of XR experiences to ensure that they are inclusive, safe and respectful of users.

2.5. Revenue sources

The advent of the metaverse is a revolution in the way companies do business. The ability to deliver immersive experiences to customers brings unparalleled added value, while opening up a wealth of avenues for revenue generation. But, to make the most of these opportunities, companies need to adapt their business models to this new environment, something that requires a thorough understanding of monetization strategies, which are unique to the metaverse.

The metaverse not only redefines the concept of online presence, it also reimagines how revenue can be generated in a digital space. Unlike traditional Web1 and Web2 strategies, the metaverse, as a representative of Web3, enables direct monetization through digital goods and services, subscriptions and memberships, advertising and sponsorship, commissions and fees, and licensing and royalties. In addition, with the adoption of blockchain technology, the opportunity arises to tokenize assets and allow end users to derive monetary benefits from their participation in the metaverse platform.

However, this wide range of options also poses a major challenge for companies. Each business model and brand objective will require a different monetization strategy. It is essential to understand these strategies and know how to implement them, in order to adapt and thrive in this new environment. At the same time, companies must keep in mind that their target audience is also undergoing this transition, which means that their expectations and behaviors are evolving.

The need to adapt to these new conditions is imperative to remain competitive in the coming years. Understanding and effectively applying new monetization and audience engagement strategies in the metaverse will change the way companies do business. It will bring new revenue streams and potentially transform the very nature of the business-to-customer relationship. In this chapter, we will explore in depth the various revenue streams available in the metaverse and how they can be leveraged to adapt and thrive in this exciting new environment.

2.5.1. Evolution of Income Sources: From Web1 to Web3

The development of digital technology and the expansion of the Internet have completely transformed the way companies generate revenue. Throughout this evolution from Web1 to Web3, new forms of monetization have been discovered, marking a transition from more traditional revenue models to newer, more innovative methods.

In the early days of the Web1, most companies generated revenue in very traditional ways: sales of goods or services, impression-based advertising and, in some cases, subscriptions. This stage was dominated by a one-way model, with companies offering content and services to users, who passively consumed what was offered.

With the advent of Web2, digital business models became more sophisticated. New forms of interaction were introduced, and with them, new ways of generating income. The rise of social networks, blogs and other forms of user-generated content enabled companies to monetize user attention and data, giving rise to revenue models based on targeted advertising and data sales. In addition, the app economy and the popularity of online stores opened up new possibilities for the sale of digital goods and services.

In today's Web3 and metaverse, the boundaries between users and content providers are blurring even further. Users can now be both consumers and creators, and can even own parts of the digital ecosystem in which they participate. This has opened up new ways of generating revenue, such as the sale of non-fungible tokens (NFTs), the token economy and smart contracts. Companies can now monetize almost any aspect of the digital experience, from virtual property to user interactions, and can benefit from the increasing decentralization and tokenization of the digital economy.

This shift toward more complex and decentralized forms of monetization in the Web3 and metaverse poses both challenges and opportunities for companies. While these new forms of revenue generation may be more difficult to manage and understand, they also offer the potential to diversify revenue streams and create more resilient and sustainable business models. In the following sections, we will further explain these new forms of revenue generation and how they can be leveraged in the metaverse.

2.5.2. Sale of Digital Goods and Services

The sale of digital goods and services has become one of the main sources of revenue in the metaverse. This monetization model takes advantage of the unique capabilities of virtual environments, where objects and services are not subject to the physical constraints of the real world.

Digital assets can take many forms, from being virtual objects in a video game to non-fungible tokens (NFTs) representing ownership of a digital artwork. These goods can be bought and sold in the metaverse, allowing companies to monetize their digital content in ways that would be impossible in a physical environment. For example, a fashion designer could sell digital versions of their clothes, for users to wear on their avatar in the metaverse.

In addition to digital goods, digital services also represent an important source of revenue. These services can range from performing specific tasks in a virtual environment to offering immersive and personalized experiences. For example, a travel company could offer virtual tours to exotic destinations, or a yoga teacher could teach classes on a virtual beach.

However, for the successful sale of digital goods and services, it is crucial to understand the expectations and needs of your target audience in the metaverse. This means paying attention to usability and accessibility aspects, as well as to the quality and originality of your goods and services. You will also need to consider the legal and ethical issues associated with the sale of digital goods and services, such as intellectual property and privacy issues.

In summary, selling digital goods and services in the metaverse offers great opportunities to generate revenue, but it also requires a deep understanding of your audience and a careful approach to user experience.

Case of Success in the Sale of Digital Goods and Services: CryptoKitties

An emblematic success story in the sale of digital assets is that of CryptoKitties. This blockchain-based game, launched in 2017, allows users to buy, collect, breed and sell virtual cats called "CryptoKitties". Each Crypto Kitty is a non-fungible token (NFT) on the Ethereum network, meaning it is unique and irreplaceable.

CryptoKitties has demonstrated the possibility of giving value to unique and collectible virtual objects. Users are willing to pay significant amounts of cryptocurrencies to own these digital cats, some of which have even sold for more than $100,000.

The success of CryptoKitties lies in several factors. First, the game leverages blockchain technology to create digital goods that are unique and scarce. This gives CryptoKitties tangible value and ownership, despite their digital nature. Secondly, the game is accessible, with an attractive design and easy-to-understand game mechanics. This has helped CryptoKitties appeal to a wide range of users beyond cryptocurrency enthusiasts.

Finally, CryptoKitties has been able to generate a sense of community and belonging among its users. CryptoKitties owners often form emotional bonds with their virtual cats, and enjoy the opportunity to interact and compete with other users in breeding and trading CryptoKitties.

In short, CryptoKitties is an excellent example of how digital assets can be monetized in the metaverse. It demonstrates that with the right technology and a user-centric approach, it is possible to generate significant revenue through the sale of digital goods and services.

2.5.3. Subscriptions and Memberships

Subscriptions and memberships represent another important source of revenue in the metaverse. Similar to Web 2.0 business models, these can provide a steady and predictable revenue stream for companies and projects in the metaverse.

The basic idea of this model is to offer users access to exclusive content, services, benefits or experiences in exchange for a regular payment, usually monthly or annually. Subscriptions and memberships can vary in cost and level of access, allowing companies to segment their offerings and maximize their revenue potential.

This model is particularly effective in the metaverse, where immersive and personalized experiences are highly valued. Examples of subscription benefits in the metaverse may include access to exclusive areas, special skills or items, priority assistance, or even the ability to influence the development and direction of the community or virtual world.

It is important to note that, to be successful with this revenue model, the subscription or membership offering must provide real and measurable value to users. This can be achieved through a combination of high-quality, unique content, useful benefits and a strong sense of community and belonging.

Subscriptions and memberships can also be used in combination with other revenue models, such as the sale of digital goods, advertising and sponsorship, to diversify and increase revenues. This can help metaverse companies remain financially stable and resilient in the face of market fluctuations.

In summary, subscriptions and memberships represent a valuable opportunity for companies and projects in the metaverse to generate revenue in a sustainable way, while offering users access to exclusive and personalized experiences.

Inspirational Example: Premium Membership in a Metaverse Educational Platform

Imagine an educational platform in the metaverse, allowing its users to access immersive learning experiences. Classes could address a variety of topics, from science and technology to history and literature, and could be taught by subject matter experts from around the world.

The platform could offer a premium membership option, providing users with additional value beyond the standard learning experience. Premium members may have priority access to new classes and programs, one-on-one mentoring sessions with instructors, and the opportunity to request customized class topics. In addition, they could get discounts on other goods and services within the metaverse, such as digital books and study tools.

In addition, the platform could offer incentives for premium member interaction and engagement. For example, they could receive rewards for completing certain tasks or achievements, which they could redeem for other goods and services within the metaverse.

To monetize this premium membership, the platform could charge a monthly or annual fee. This would provide a steady and predictable source of revenue, while fostering long-term user loyalty and engagement.

This type of membership model could be very successful in the metaverse, as it would combine the convenience and accessibility of online education with the immersion and interactivity of virtual reality. At the same time, it would offer users additional value and an enriching experience, which could contribute to a high user retention and satisfaction rate.

2.5.4. Advertising and Sponsorship

Advertising and sponsorship represent very traditional forms of revenue generation, which have evolved with the emergence of the metaverse. Now, these strategies represent a new level of interactivity and engagement, creating new opportunities for brands and advertisers.

Advertising in the metaverse involves the promotion of products or services in virtual environments through different formats. These can range from immersive ads, where users interact with products in a three-dimensional environment, to the insertion of advertising in high-traffic spaces, such as virtual plazas, shopping malls, or real-time events.

Augmented reality presents new forms of advertising, where products can be promoted in the user's physical reality through AR devices, creating an interaction between the physical and virtual worlds.

On the other hand, **sponsorship** in the metaverse refers to collaboration between brands and metaverse platforms, or collaborating with content creators within the metaverse. Brands can sponsor events, builds, or experiences within these platforms, allowing them to increase their visibility and reach audiences in a direct and meaningful way.

Advertising and sponsorship revenues can vary widely, depending on factors such as the popularity of the metaverse platform, the amount and type of traffic it attracts, and the level of audience engagement. As the metaverse continues to grow and develop, advertising and sponsorship opportunities are expected to continue to evolve and expand, providing companies with new ways to reach their target audiences and generate revenue.

In addition, it is worth noting that advertisers can leverage the immersive and social nature of the metaverse to create more engaging and interactive advertising campaigns. For example, they can design advertising experiences that invite users to interact with products virtually, either by trying them out, customizing them or sharing them with their friends within the platform.

On the other hand, sponsorship can take various forms in the metaverse. An example might be a brand sponsoring the construction of an iconic building or public space on a metaverse platform, or collaborating with a popular content creator to promote their products or services.

It is important to keep in mind that, unlike traditional advertising, advertising and sponsorship in the metaverse must be subtle and organic, to avoid disrupting the immersive user experience. Therefore, advertising and sponsorship strategies must be carefully considered and adapted to the expectations and behaviors of the target audience.

Finally, as with all revenue streams in the metaverse, it is critical to keep up with the latest trends and technological advances, and be willing to innovate and experiment to find the advertising and sponsorship strategies that best suit your business.

Inspirational example: Mercedes-Benz

Let's suppose that the prestigious luxury car brand, Mercedes-Benz, decides to enter the metaverse to establish a new channel of interaction with its audience. Instead of simply recreating a digital showroom, the brand opted for a more innovative and disruptive strategy.

In its metaverse, Mercedes-Benz creates a fully immersive experience that goes beyond the simple car showroom. Visitors can attend virtual presentations of the new models, where each car is displayed in unique and dynamic scenarios, changing according to the characteristics and personality of the car. They can even "drive" these cars in hyper-realistic virtual environments, experiencing first-hand the feeling of luxury and performance that Mercedes-Benz is known for.

To promote this innovative space, the brand decided to collaborate with digital celebrities in the metaverse. It invites e-sports stars, for example, to compete in virtual races using its new models. These events are broadcast live in the metaverse and on social networks, generating a large number of viewers and participants.

This approach would not only promote the Mercedes-Benz brand and its products in a virtual space, but also create a significant revenue stream through advertising and sponsorship. Luxury and performance product brands, for example, might be interested in sponsoring these events and showcasing their products in this space, creating a mutually beneficial synergy.

Of course, this is a hypothetical scenario, but it reflects the immense possibilities that the metaverse can offer for brands willing to explore new territories and reinvent the way they interact with their audience.

2.5.5. Commissions and Fees

Commissions and fees are another significant source of income in the metaverse. This monetization model is especially relevant for platforms that act as intermediaries between different parties, whether between buyers and sellers of digital goods, between companies and consumers, or between content creators and their audience.

A typical example of this model on the Web2 are e-commerce platforms, which charge a fee for each transaction made on their site. In the metaverse, this model can be expanded to a wide range of interactions and transactions. For example, a metaverse marketplace that allows users to buy, sell and trade virtual goods can generate revenue through commissions on transactions made on its platform.

In addition, the implementation of blockchain technology and cryptocurrencies in the metaverse opens up the possibility of microtransactions, allowing platforms to charge small fees for a large number of interactions and transactions. For example, a platform could charge a small fee for access to exclusive areas, for the use of certain functionalities, or for participation in events or activities.

Finally, it is crucial that rates and commissions are aligned with the expectations and behavior of the target audience. Users should perceive sufficient value in the interactions or transactions for which they are paying, and fees and commissions should neither be prohibitive nor deter users from participating in the platform. Otherwise, this monetization model can backfire, reducing user activity and ultimately platform revenue.

Successful implementation of commissions and fees in the metaverse requires a thorough understanding of users, a clear and compelling value proposition, and a well-defined pricing and monetization strategy.

2.5.6. Licenses and Royalties

Licensing and royalties are a highly effective source of revenue in the metaverse, especially with the increasing prevalence of the tokenized economy and digital property.

Licensing is a legal agreement whereby one party (the licensor) allows another (the licensee) to use its property (in this case, digital goods, software, technology, etc.), in exchange for monetary compensation. This compensation may be a one-time payment, periodic payments or a combination of both.

Royalties, on the other hand, are a type of license where compensation is based on the use or sales of the licensed property. Royalties are common in the music and entertainment industry, but they are also increasingly relevant in the metaverse as content creators look for ways to monetize their work.

In the metaverse, licenses and royalties can take many different forms. For example, a digital artist could license his work to an owner of a virtual space for exhibition, and receive royalties every time someone buys a digital copy of his work. Similarly, a software company could license its virtual reality technology to a game developer, and receive a percentage of the game's sales.

In addition, blockchain technology and smart contracts can make licensing and royalty management more efficient and transparent. For example, a smart contract could automate royalty payments so that each time a transaction is made with the licensed property, a portion of that transaction is automatically redirected to the rights holder.

It is important to note that licenses and royalties must be carefully managed to protect proprietary rights, and to ensure that all parties involved receive fair compensation. This may require the advice of legal and financial experts and a thorough understanding of the relevant laws and regulations.

Inspirational example: LEGO in the Metaverse

Let's imagine for a moment LEGO, the well-known Danish toy company, venturing into the metaverse and adapting its business model to take advantage of licensing and royalties.

LEGO could create a "LEGO Metaverse," a virtual reality platform where users could buy, build and explore digital worlds made entirely of LEGO blocks. As in the real world, users would have to purchase digital LEGO blocks to build their own creations. These blocks could be licensed to users for a set price, generating a direct revenue stream for LEGO.

But, LEGO could also go further, and set up a royalty system. For example, they could allow users to sell or rent their

LEGO creations to other users. Each time a transaction took place, a portion of the sale or rental price would automatically be redirected to LEGO as a royalty. In this way, LEGO would not only monetize the initial sale of digital blocks, but also the secondary transactions made by users.

In addition, LEGO could expand its licensing system through collaborations with other brands and franchises. For example, they could collaborate with Marvel to launch a series of digital LEGO blocks of superheroes, or with Disney to create a digital princess castle. These collaborations would not only generate new revenue streams for LEGO, but would also increase the attractiveness of its metaverse and attract more users.

This example illustrates how companies can use licensing and royalties to generate revenue in the metaverse, adapting their existing business models and taking advantage of the new opportunities offered by the digital economy. However, it also underscores the need for careful management and strategic planning to ensure that these revenue streams are sustainable and beneficial to all parties involved.

2.5.7. Tokenization of Assets and User Benefits

Asset tokenization and monetization of user benefits are two revenue generation mechanisms that are inherently unique to the metaverse and Web3. Both harness the power of blockchain and smart contracts to create new forms of value and profit in the metaverse.

Asset tokenization involves the digital representation of a physical or digital asset on the blockchain. These tokens can be exchanged, sold or bought in the metaverse, creating a secondary market for digital assets. For example, a company could tokenize a number of unique virtual buildings in its metaverse, and then sell these tokens to users. As more users entered the metaverse and demand for these buildings grew, the value of the tokens could also increase.

In addition, tokenization allows companies to implement fractional ownership systems, where multiple parties can own a portion of a digital asset. This can create new investment opportunities and allow users to access assets that would otherwise be beyond their financial reach.

Meanwhile, monetization of user benefits involves allowing users to earn tokens or cryptocurrencies through their interactions and contributions in the metaverse. For example, a user can earn tokens for building impressive structures, contributing to the platform's code, moderating communities or even just for actively participating. These tokens can be exchanged for goods and services within the metaverse, sold on a secondary market, or converted into fiat currency.

Both mechanisms allow companies to generate revenue, either through the initial sale of tokens, or through commissions and fees on secondary transactions. However, they also benefit users by allowing them to own and benefit from their contributions to the metaverse. This can encourage greater participation and engagement, creating a virtuous cycle that benefits both companies and users.

Inspirational example: ZARA and Tokenized Fashion

Leading fashion brands like ZARA could leverage asset tokenization to revolutionize the fashion world in the metaverse.

Suppose ZARA decides to launch a digital clothing line exclusively for the metaverse. These digital garments could be tokenized and sold to users in the metaverse. To make it even more interesting, ZARA could decide to make these garments "unique pieces", meaning that there is only one token for each garment. This exclusivity could add additional value to the garments, making users willing to pay a premium price.

In addition, ZARA could implement a fractional ownership system for its most exclusive garments. For example, a piece of digital couture created by a famous designer could be tokenized and its ownership divided among several users. This would allow users who cannot afford to buy the complete part to have a fraction of the ownership of the part. In addition, these users could exchange, sell or buy fractions of these pieces in the secondary market.

In addition to generating revenue through the sale of these tokens, ZARA could also benefit from the fees and commissions charged on secondary market transactions. On the other hand, users could benefit by being able to access exclusive and unique garments, and by being able to earn money through their investments in digital fashion.

This model would not only allow ZARA to diversify and increase its revenue sources, but could also reinforce its brand image as a leader in fashion innovation. At the same time, it could provide users with a new way to interact and benefit from fashion in the metaverse.

2.5.8. Monetization Strategies According to Brand Objectives

In the metaverse, as in any other business environment, monetization strategies must be aligned with overall brand objectives. Not all brands enter the metaverse with the same purpose; while some may seek direct revenue generation through the sale of goods and services, others may be more focused on brand building and customer interaction. Each objective will require a different monetization strategy.

Direct Sales: If the goal is to generate revenue through the sale of goods and services, brands could consider strategies such as creating and selling digital goods and services, implementing subscriptions and memberships, or tokenizing assets. These strategies allow brands to generate direct revenue from their customers.

Brand Building and Customer Engagement: If the primary objective is to build brand and increase customer engagement, brands can consider advertising and sponsorship in the metaverse. While these strategies may not generate direct revenue, they can increase brand visibility and customer loyalty, which can translate into higher revenue in the long run.

Community Building and User Participation: If the brand aims to build a strong and engaged community in the metaverse, they might consider strategies that allow users to benefit financially from their participation. This could include tokenizing assets that users can own, buy and sell, or implementing a reward system to incentivize user participation.

Ultimately, the choice of monetization strategies in the metaverse should be a reflection of the brand's objectives and the expectations and behaviors of its target audience. Brands must experiment and adapt their strategies as the metaverse evolves to ensure they are maximizing revenue and meeting their objectives.

2.6. Key metrics

Immersion in the metaverse implies a profound transformation in the way we interact with users and, therefore, in how we measure those interactions. This three-dimensional and interactive environment, which crosses the boundaries of the physical and digital, demands new metrics and methods to analyze and understand user behaviors and preferences. As in other digital channels, monitoring and analyzing key metrics is crucial to understand the performance of our actions and be able to make informed decisions that allow us to achieve our business objectives.

However, we cannot simply move traditional Web2 metrics into the metaverse, as we must be prepared to understand and leverage the metrics that are intrinsic to this new environment. Some of these metrics may be related to mobility and interactions within the metaverse, users' ability to interact with three-dimensional objects, immersion and participation in shared experiences, among others.

In addition, it is important to remember that the metaverse is just another channel in our multichannel strategy, so our key metrics in this channel must be aligned with the general KPIs of our strategy and contribute to the achievement of our overall objectives.

Finally, it is foreseeable that new metrics and analysis tools will emerge over time as the adoption and development of the metaverse progresses. We must therefore be alert to these developments and be ready to adapt our measurement strategies as they occur.

Chapter 2.6, which follows, will provide you with a detailed understanding of the key metrics in the metaverse, from their basic concepts to their application in different scenarios and how to use them to optimize your strategies.

2.6.1. Basic Concepts: Metrics and Indicators

The performance of a business or marketing campaign in the metaverse, as in any other environment, needs to be systematically measured and evaluated in order to make informed and effective decisions. This is where the concepts of metrics and indicators come into play.

Metrics: Metrics are quantitative or qualitative values that can be measured and that provide information about a specific aspect of performance. Some common examples include the number of active users, conversion rate, average time spent on the platform, among others. They are the basis for building more complex and valuable indicators for the analysis of a company's performance.

Indicators: Indicators, or **key performance indicators** (KPIs), are selected metrics that represent critical factors for the success of a business. These indicators provide a more in-depth and goal-oriented assessment of business performance. For example, in the context of the metaverse, customer acquisition cost (CAC) and customer lifetime value (CLV) are two key indicators for companies seeking to optimize their investments and maximize their profits.

It is important to note that both metrics and indicators must be relevant, measurable and actionable for the business. They should be carefully selected and regularly monitored to provide a clear picture of business performance and guide decision making.

Finally, metrics and indicators should not be viewed as static entities. As the business and the metaverse evolve, metrics and indicators will also need to adapt to remain relevant and useful. In the following sections, we will delve more deeply into how these concepts apply to the metaverse and how they can help companies achieve their business objectives.

2.6.2. Metrics and Indicators in the Metaverse Context

Within the metaverse, both metrics and indicators become even more relevant, given the interactive and dynamic nature of this new digital environment. In addition to the traditional metrics used on the Web1 and Web2, such as visitor traffic or conversion rate, there are new metrics specific to the metaverse that offer deeper insight into user behavior and interactions.

Some of the key metrics in the metaverse could include:

1. **Active users**: As with any digital platform, the number of active users is a key indicator of popularity and participation in your metaverse space.

2. **Time of permanence**: Given the immersive nature of the metaverse, the time users spend in your space can be a valuable indicator of their engagement and satisfaction.

3. **Interactions per visit**: This indicator can give insight into how users interact with the environment and with other users, providing useful insight into the functionality and attractiveness of your space.

4. **Transactions of digital goods and services**: If your business in the metaverse involves the sale or exchange of digital goods and services, tracking these transactions is crucial to measuring financial success.

On the other hand, key performance indicators in the metaverse could be:

1. **Customer Acquisition Cost (CAC)**: This indicator can help you understand how much it costs to attract a new customer to your metaverse space.

2. **Customer Lifetime Value (CLV)**: As with any business, calculating CLV in the metaverse can provide valuable insight into the long-term value of your customers and the profitability of your acquisition efforts.

3. **User retention rate**: This indicator can give an idea of how many users return to your metaverse space after their first visit, providing a measure of user engagement and loyalty.

4. **Interactions with the brand**: Whether your goal is to build brand awareness or promote a product or service, tracking interactions with brand elements can be a useful indicator of the success of your marketing efforts.

2.6.3. Key General Metrics in the Metaverse

In the metaverse, certain general metrics are essential to understand user behavior and trends. These metrics provide a broad view of overall performance and are fundamental to any type of presence in the metaverse, whether for commercial, marketing or community purposes.

1. **Active users**: This is the number of users interacting in a specific metaverse space in a given period of time. This metric allows us to understand the popularity of such a space and the frequency of interactions.

2. **Time of permanence**: This metric measures the time users spend in a space or interact with a specific activity. Longer dwell time may mean greater user engagement with the content or activities provided.

3. **Interactions per user**: Measures the number of interactions a user makes during a visit. These interactions can range from movement and exploration, to more meaningful interactions such as the purchase of a good or service, or interaction with other users.

4. **User return rate**: This metric tracks the percentage of users who return to your site after their first visit. A high return rate can indicate that users find value in your space and are engaged with your value proposition.

5. **Virtual/augmented/mixed reality interactions**: Since the metaverse enables immersive experiences, measuring specific virtual, augmented or mixed reality interactions can provide valuable insights into how users engage with these technologies.

6. **Conversion rate**: As in any digital environment, conversion rate, i.e. the percentage of visitors who take a desired action (such as a purchase or subscription), is critical to measuring success.

2.6.4. Specific Metrics for Product or Service Businesses in the Metaverse

If your presence in the metaverse includes selling products or services, whether tangible or digital, there are several key metrics you can consider to evaluate the performance of your offerings.

1. **Total sales**: This metric reflects the total number of products or services sold during a specific period of time.

2. **Revenue per product or service**: This metric shows how much revenue each individual product or service is generating.

3. **Average Order Value (AOV)**: This metric reflects the average amount users spend on each transaction.

4. **Cost per acquisition (CPA)**: The CPA reflects how much it costs, on average, to acquire a new customer. It is calculated by dividing total marketing and sales costs by the number of new customers acquired.

5. **Return on investment (ROI)**: ROI is a crucial metric to evaluate the efficiency of your investments. It is calculated as the net profit divided by the total investment and is generally expressed as a percentage.

6. **Shopping cart abandonment rate**: This metric indicates the percentage of users who add products to their shopping cart but abandon the purchase process before completing it.

7. **Frequency of purchase**: This metric reflects the number of times an average customer makes a purchase during a specific time period.

8. **Customer Life Cycle Value (CLV)**: The CLV is a forecast of the total net revenue attributed to the entire future relationship with a customer.

2.6.5. Specific Metrics for Marketing Campaigns in the Metaverse

In the context of a metaverse marketing campaign, it is crucial to measure its performance and effectiveness through appropriate metrics and KPIs. These are some of the most important ones:

1. **Scope**: This metric shows the total number of unique users who have viewed or interacted with your marketing campaign.

2. **Impressions**: This metric reflects the total number of times your marketing campaign has been viewed, regardless of whether or not users have interacted with it.

3. **Interactions**: This metric reflects the number of interactions users have had with your marketing campaign. This may include clicks, "likes", comments, shares, among others.

4. **Conversion rate**: This metric reflects the percentage of users who have taken the desired action after viewing or interacting with your marketing campaign. The "desired action" may vary, depending on the objectives of your campaign.

5. **Return on advertising investment (ROAS)**: ROAS reflects the financial return on each euro invested in the marketing campaign. It is calculated by dividing the income obtained from the advertising campaign by the total cost of the campaign.

6. **Time dedicated to interaction**: This metric reflects the average time users spend interacting with your marketing campaign. This is an especially important metric in the metaverse, where immersive experiences can retain users for longer periods of time.

7. **User Experience (UX)**: Although not a quantitative metric per se, UX is a critical factor in evaluating the success of a marketing campaign in the metaverse. This can be measured through user satisfaction surveys and analysis of user comments and feedback.

Metaverse marketing campaigns, due to their immersive and multidimensional nature, may require the application of a broader and more diverse set of metrics compared to traditional marketing campaigns. However, as with any other marketing strategy, careful monitoring and analysis of these metrics will allow you to continually adjust and improve your campaign to get the best possible results.

2.6.6. How to Monitor and Use the Key Metrics

Always keep in mind that the purpose of metrics is to explain what has happened, and with the right context, key insights can be obtained to improve actions and get closer to the objectives.

But not everything goes, here we provide you with a series of steps to follow to get the most out of your key metrics:

1. **Definition of Key Metrics**: The first step is to define what your key metrics will be. These should be aligned with your business objectives or marketing campaign and should be able to provide a clear measure of your performance and progress.

2. **Follow-up tools**: You will need appropriate tracking and analysis tools to collect and analyze your key metrics. Many metaverse platforms provide built-in analysis tools, but you can also use third-party analysis tools that specialize in the metaverse.

3. **Data collection**: Collect your metrics on a regular basis. Depending on your objectives and the metrics you are tracking, you may need to collect data on a daily, weekly or monthly basis.

4. **Metrics analysis**: Once you have collected your metrics, you should analyze them to get a clear understanding of what they mean. Identify trends, observe changes and evaluate your performance in relation to your goals and objectives.

5. **Adjustments and improvements**: Use the conclusions of your metrics analysis to make adjustments and improvements to your business strategy or marketing campaign. This may involve adjusting your content, changing your targeting approach, improving the user experience or any number of other possible actions.

6. **Continuous evaluation**: The monitoring and use of key metrics is an ongoing process. You should continually look at your metrics and use the results to improve and grow. Over time, you will know how you need to change your key metrics as your objectives evolve or as new opportunities or challenges arise.

Remember that metrics and indicators are only part of the equation. They should be used in combination with other data and a deep understanding of your audience and the metaverse market to get a complete picture of your company's performance and potential.

2.7. NFT

NFTs, or non-fungible tokens, are more than just digital artwork, available on trading platforms such as Open Sea. In the context of the metaverse and the emerging Web3 economy, NFTs represent a fundamental shift in how value is created, distributed and exchanged.

NFTs are unique digital assets on the blockchain, representing ownership of a specific object or resource. This can cover a wide range of items, not only works of art, but also virtual properties, digital identities, copyrights and much more. Unlike fungible tokens, such as cryptocurrencies, each NFT is unique and irreplaceable, providing a mechanism for proof of ownership and authenticity in the digital world.

But why is this relevant for companies entering the metaverse? NFTs open up a new world of possibilities for monetization, user engagement and marketing strategies. With NFTs, companies can create exclusive and non-transferable experiences, from collectibles and limited edition products to VIP access to events and experiences in the metaverse.

In addition, NFTs allow companies to take advantage of the inherent benefits of blockchain, which include transparency, security and traceability. This can increase user trust, enable new forms of interaction and engagement, and create opportunities for innovation in business models.

Finally, and perhaps most importantly, NFTs can be a powerful driver of audience engagement on the Web3, and surpass the levels achieved on the Web2. By enabling users to own and control their digital assets and experiences, NFTs can generate a sense of belonging, engagement and loyalty that goes beyond traditional digital interactions.

In short, NFTs are an essential part of the metaverse economy and the emerging Web3. However, their potential goes beyond digital artwork: they represent a new way to generate and distribute value, deliver unique and engaging experiences, and connect with users on a deeper level. In the following subchapters, we will explore these topics in more depth, starting with an explanation of **what exactly NFTs are** in Chapter 2.7.1.

2.7.1. What are NFTs?

NFTs, meaning Non-Fungible Tokens, are a special class of digital assets. Unlike cryptocurrencies such as Bitcoin or Ethereum, which are fungible and can be exchanged one for one, NFTs are unique and irreplaceable, i.e., they are not identically exchangeable.

Each NFT is a unique digital object that can be uniquely identified. This means that each NFT has information or characteristics that differentiate them from each other, which gives them their value and uniqueness. These characteristics may include data on ownership, authenticity, rarity, location, and other relevant attributes that are recorded on a blockchain.

A relevant aspect of NFTs is that they are tokenizable, meaning that any type of asset, whether physical or digital, can be converted into an NFT on the blockchain. This feature allows the creation of a digital certificate of ownership, which can be bought, sold or exchanged in the metaverse or on blockchain platforms.

NFTs have become largely popular in the field of digital art, but their application goes far beyond that. In the metaverse, NFTs can represent a wide variety of goods and services, including, but not limited to, collectibles, virtual property, copyrights and identities. Their versatility and ability to provide irrefutable proof of ownership and authenticity make them a valuable tool for business and marketing strategies in the metaverse.

2.7.2. Uses of NFTs in the Metaverse

In the metaverse, NFTs are used for a variety of purposes, which go far beyond the boundaries of traditional digital environments. Below, we highlight some of the most innovative and promising uses of NFTs in the metaverse:

1. **Virtual property**: NFTs enable the purchase, sale and trade of virtual real estate. This can range from acquiring virtual parcels of land, buildings or even entire worlds within a metaverse. The owners of these assets may have ownership rights over them, as well as the ability to customize or monetize them.

2. **Art and Collectibles**: Artists can tokenize their artwork as NFTs, guaranteeing its authenticity and enabling the sale and trade of their artwork in the metaverse. Similarly, virtual collectibles, such as trading cards or unique avatars, can be tokenized as NFTs, allowing users to own and trade these items in a secure manner.

3. **Copyright and Intellectual Property**: NFTs can also be used to tokenize and manage copyrights and intellectual property in the metaverse. This can range from music and videos, to patents and trademarks, allowing creators and rights owners to receive compensation for the use of their works.

4. **Virtual Identities**: NFTs can be used to represent and verify identities in the metaverse. This can allow users to have more secure and private control over their virtual identity, as well as facilitate more secure transactions.

5. **Exclusive Services**: NFTs can be used to offer exclusive services in the metaverse. For example, an NFT could give its owner access to special events, premium content, networking opportunities and more.

6. **Gaming Assets**: NFTs are also being used to tokenize gaming assets in the metaverse, allowing players to securely own and trade these assets. This can include everything from game elements to characters and skills.

Inspirational example: Nike in the Metaverse

Let's imagine that the well-known sports brand Nike decides to carry out a marketing action in the metaverse, taking advantage of the potential of NFTs.

The action consists of the creation of a "Nike Metaverse Stadium", a virtual stadium where users can interact with the brand and its products in innovative ways. Within this space, Nike could sell NFTs representing digital versions of its most iconic products, such as its limited edition sneakers. Users could purchase these NFTs to use on their avatars in the metaverse, allowing them to "wear" their favorite Nike sneakers in the virtual environment.

But the potential of NFTs goes beyond simple product representation. Nike could also use NFTs to grant users access to exclusive experiences in the "Nike Metaverse Stadium." For example, they could sell NFTs that grant the right to participate in virtual sporting events, such as races or high jump competitions, or interact with Nike-sponsored athletes in the metaverse. Users may even have the opportunity to win exclusive NFTs through their participation in these events.

The value of this marketing action lies in its ability to connect with users in the metaverse in new and exciting ways. By using NFTs, Nike could not only increase the visibility of its products, but also foster user loyalty and engagement by offering unique and valuable experiences in the metaverse. At the same time, the sale of NFTs would represent a new source of revenue for the brand.

In short, Nike, by integrating NFTs into its metaverse marketing strategy, would be innovating the way it interacts and connects with its consumers, creating a more immersive, personalized and rewarding experience.

2.7.3. Revenue Generation with NFTs

NFTs offer a wide range of opportunities for revenue generation in the metaverse. Their ability to create and represent value in a virtual environment makes them a highly effective tool for monetizing digital assets and experiences. Below, we describe some of the most promising strategies for generating revenue with NFTs in the metaverse:

1. **Sale of Virtual Goods**: NFTs can be used to sell a variety of virtual goods, from digital art objects to virtual properties. Creators can tokenize their works and sell them directly to consumers, allowing them to retain a

greater share of the profits compared to traditional sales channels.

2. **Trade and Resale**: NFTs, by their unique and irreplaceable nature, have significant potential for resale. Users can buy and sell NFTs in virtual markets, generating profits from price fluctuations.

3. **Collection of Royalties**: When an NFT is sold, the original creator of the NFT may receive a portion of the sale in the form of royalties. This can provide a continuous and passive source of income for creators.

4. **Access to Exclusive Content or Experiences**: NFTs can be used to grant access to exclusive content or experiences in the metaverse, which can generate additional revenue. This can include access to virtual events, premium content, networking opportunities and more.

5. **Participation in the Game**: NFTs can be used to monetize participation in games in the metaverse. Players can buy, sell or exchange game assets in the form of NFTs, and companies can earn a commission from these transactions.

6. **Customization Services**: NFTs can offer opportunities for personalization services, such as customization of avatars or virtual spaces. Users can pay for NFTs that allow them to customize their experience in the metaverse, which can generate revenue for the companies offering these services.

These strategies represent only a fraction of the potential that NFTs have to generate revenue in the metaverse. As this technology continues to evolve, new monetization opportunities are likely to emerge.

Inspirational example: Marvel in the Metaverse

We could imagine a scenario in which the well-known Marvel comic book and movie franchise decides to venture into the metaverse, using NFTs as a means to generate revenue and provide a unique experience for fans.

Marvel's strategy could involve the creation of an interactive and dynamic "Marvel Metaverse Universe" where fans could explore and immerse themselves in their favorite stories and characters in a completely new way. Here, Marvel could sell NFTs representing iconic elements of its franchises.

For example, Marvel could sell unique digital comic book NFTs, which would grant holders exclusive rights to special or limited editions. These comics could contain unique art and narratives, which would make them very valuable to collectors.

In addition, Marvel could generate revenue through the sale of NFTs representing "experiences" in the metaverse. For example, an NFT could grant its holder the opportunity to join the Avengers on a virtual mission or have a face-to-face encounter with iconic characters such as Iron Man or Black Widow in the metaverse.

Another option could be the sale of NFTs representing exclusive virtual "gear," such as Captain America's shield or Iron Man's suit, which users could use to customize their avatars.

These NFTs would not only provide Marvel with a new revenue stream, but would also allow fans to interact with the brand in entirely new and exciting ways, increasing their long-term engagement and loyalty. In short, Marvel would be at the forefront of marketing and monetization innovation in the metaverse through the strategic use of NFTs.

2.7.4. NFTs and User Experience

NFTs not only represent a novel source of revenue for companies in the metaverse, but also have the potential to substantially improve the user experience.

NFTs, in essence, are unique digital assets that can be owned by users in the metaverse. They can represent a variety of goods and services, from works of art and collectibles to virtual identities and property rights. By owning these unique and irreplaceable elements, users have the opportunity to personalize their experience in the metaverse, which can increase their engagement and satisfaction.

In addition, NFTs can facilitate greater interaction between users and brands. For example, a company could issue NFTs that grant users exclusive access to unique experiences, products or services in the metaverse, such as special events, exclusive content or even private areas within the metaverse environment. Not only can this increase user loyalty and engagement, but it can also provide companies with valuable opportunities to get their feedback and learn more about their customers.

Another aspect to consider is user empowerment through ownership of NFTs. Users are not only consumers in the metaverse, but can also become creators and sellers of their own digital content. Some companies are already experimenting with business models that allow users to create and sell their own NFTs, which can provide users with a source of revenue and a greater sense of participation and ownership in the metaverse.

In summary, integrating NFTs into the business strategy in the metaverse can significantly improve the user experience by providing opportunities for personalization, interaction with brands and active participation in the digital economy of the metaverse.

Inspirational Example: Disney and the User Experience with NFTs in the Metaverse

Disney, known for its commitment to magic and immersive experience, could be one of the brands that could successfully leverage NFTs to enhance the user experience in the metaverse. Imagine a Disney metaverse where fans can explore and experience their favorite movies, characters and theme parks in entirely new and interactive ways.

Disney could issue NFTs representing digital tickets to exclusive virtual experiences, such as a VIP tour of Cinderella's castle or an expedition through The Lion King's Pridelands, all in the comfort of your home. These NFTs would not only provide users with access to unique experiences, but could also be collected and exchanged, creating a sense of ownership and achievement.

In addition, Disney could allow users to create and sell their own NFTs based on Disney's vast library of characters and content. For example, a talented user could create an original Mickey Mouse design and sell it as an NFT in the Disney metaverse. This would not only provide a source of revenue for creative users, but would also encourage greater participation and engagement with the brand.

Disney already has a community of passionate and committed fans. By integrating NFTs into its metaverse strategy, the company would have the opportunity to take its interaction with fans to a new level, fostering greater loyalty and long-term engagement.

2.7.5. Creation and Commercialization of NFTs

Creating and marketing NFTs in the metaverse requires a thorough understanding of both the inherent value of these digital assets and the legal and technological framework surrounding them.

First, it is important to understand that NFTs are unique cryptographic tokens that cannot be exchanged one-for-one like traditional cryptocurrencies. Each NFT contains specific information or content that is stored in a smart contract, ensuring its authenticity and ownership. This means that NFTs can represent a variety of digital goods and services, from works of art and music to virtual properties and copyrights.

The creation of an NFT involves the digitization of an asset, its tokenization through a smart contract and its publication on a blockchain. This process can be performed by individuals with technical expertise or through platforms that facilitate the creation of NFTs. It is important to remember that the creation of an NFT may also involve legal issues, such as copyright and intellectual property protection, which should be carefully considered.

The commercialization of NFTs can be done through a variety of channels. NFT marketplaces, such as Open Sea, Rarible and NBA Top Shot, allow users to buy, sell and trade NFTs. In addition, companies can integrate NFTs into their business model in the metaverse, offering them as rewards for user participation, as part of subscriptions or memberships, or as a way to access exclusive experiences or services.

Finally, it is crucial to remember that the commercialization of NFTs must be conducted in an ethical and sustainable manner. This includes respect for copyright and intellectual property rights, transparency in transactions and consideration of the environmental impact of blockchains.

In summary, the creation and commercialization of NFTs can offer new opportunities for companies in the metaverse, but it requires careful consideration and planning.

2.7.6. Challenges and Ethical Considerations around NFTs

While NFTs present an exciting opportunity to expand the metaverse economy and generate new forms of revenue and user participation, they also raise a number of challenges and ethical considerations.

1. **Intellectual Property Rights**: One of the most important challenges relates to intellectual property rights. NFTs represent unique and authentic assets, but authenticity and ownership can be difficult to prove within a digital environment. In addition, tokenization of assets involving copyrights, such as art and music, can lead to legal disputes, if proper licenses and permissions are not obtained.

2. **Fraud and Scams**: Since the NFT market is relatively new and largely unregulated, there is also a risk of fraud and scams. It is possible that counterfeit NFTs are created and sold, and that NFT prices are manipulated to defraud buyers. Education and due diligence are essential to protect against these risks.

3. **Environmental impact**: The blockchains that underpin NFTs, especially Ethereum, consume a significant amount of energy, which can contribute to climate change. Companies must take this environmental impact into account and look for ways to mitigate it, for example, by using more energy-efficient blockchains, or offsetting their carbon footprint.

4. **Inclusion and Accessibility**: NFTs have the potential to democratize access to economic opportunities in the metaverse, but they can also exacerbate inequalities if not properly managed. It is important to ensure that opportunities for participation and monetization are available to all, regardless of technical expertise or financial resources.

5. **Privacy and Security**: Finally, the commercialization of NFTs raises privacy and security issues. Personal data can be exposed on the blockchain, and NFT transactions can be vulnerable to hacking and theft. Companies must implement robust security measures and respect data protection regulations to protect users' privacy.

2.8. Competitive advantage

In the dynamic world of the metaverse, understanding and adapting the concept of competitive advantage is crucial to the success of any business. However, to meet this challenge, it is essential to re-evaluate the traditional conceptions of competitive advantage that have been used in the Web 2.0 era.

To date, competitive advantage in Web 2.0 has focused primarily on aspects such as price, quality, customer service and branding. While these elements remain relevant, the metaverse, with its immersive and user-centric nature, demands a new conceptualization of competitive advantage.

In this emerging environment, user experience and immersive experience become the key factors. Instead of focusing solely on the delivery of products or services, companies should focus on how these products or services contribute to creating meaningful and valuable immersive experiences for users.

In addition, the ability to add value in new ways becomes essential. This may include the use of emerging technologies and trends, such as virtual and augmented reality, NFTs, and real-time data, to create unique and innovative value propositions that meet the changing needs and desires of users.

2.8.1. Introduction to Competitive Advantage

Competitive advantage is a key concept in the business and marketing world. Refers to those unique attributes that enable a company to outperform its competitors. These attributes can range from product or service quality, operational efficiency, constant innovation, strong brand image, to exceptional customer service, among others. In short, any factor that differentiates you from the competition and makes customers choose you over others can be considered a competitive advantage.

A strong competitive advantage can be the cornerstone of business success. It can enable a company to dominate its industry, attract and retain more customers and earn higher profits. In addition, a sustainable competitive advantage, i.e. one that can be maintained over the long term, can protect the company from competitive threats and changes in the market environment.

However, it should be noted that competitive advantages are not static. In an ever-changing market environment, companies must continually strive to identify, develop and maintain their competitive advantages. This involves thoroughly understanding the market and customer needs, exploring and adopting innovations, and adjusting business and marketing strategy as necessary.

In the context of the metaverse, the need for competitive advantage becomes even more crucial. As companies enter this new immersive digital environment, they face a unique set of challenges and opportunities, and the ability to establish and maintain a competitive advantage could be critical to their success in the metaverse.

2.8.2. Competitive Advantage in the Metaverse Context

The metaverse, as a new domain for digital and commercial interaction, offers fertile ground for competitive advantage. But, at the same time, it poses unique challenges in terms of how companies can differentiate themselves in a space that is inherently flexible, customizable and infinite.

Competitive advantages in the metaverse derive not only from what you sell, but also from how you interact with users, how they experience your brand in this three-dimensional environment and how you make users feel part of your world.

Constant innovation is a key advantage. This can manifest itself in how you use technology and interactivity to deliver immersive and memorable experiences to your users. For example, you could be the first to use a new virtual reality feature or technology, or you could create novel and exciting user experiences that other companies have not yet explored.

Specialization can also be an advantage. In an environment where almost anything is possible, being the best at something specific can help you stand out. This could be related to the type of products or services you offer, the user experience you create, or even the specific audience you are targeting.

Collaboration is another potential competitive advantage. In the metaverse, companies can collaborate in unprecedented ways, from creating joint user experiences to integrating products and services. These collaborations can allow you to access new audiences, learn from other companies and create richer and more diverse user experiences.

Finally, operational excellence, although less visible to users, remains crucial. This includes efficiency in the creation and delivery of your products or services, the quality of your customer service and your ability to adapt quickly to changes in the metaverse environment. Companies that can operate effectively in the metaverse will be well positioned to compete and succeed.

2.8.3. Identification of Competitive Advantages in the Metaverse

Identifying competitive advantages in the metaverse requires a thorough understanding of your business, your target audience and the constantly changing environment of the metaverse. Here are some key steps and considerations to identify your competitive advantages in the metaverse:

1. **Understand your target audience**: Your audience is the heart of your business. Understand their needs, preferences and behaviors in the metaverse. What do you value? How do they interact with the metaverse? What experiences are you looking for?

2. **Analyze your strengths and opportunities**: Reflect on the unique strengths of your business and how these can be leveraged in the metaverse. It also considers emerging opportunities. Can you pioneer a new technology or interaction format? Is there an unattended niche market in the metaverse?

3. **Consider the competitive environment**: Watch your competitors in the metaverse. What are they doing right? Where are they failing? Are there unfilled spaces in the market that you can fill?

4. **Experiment and learn quickly**: The metaverse is a novel and rapidly changing environment. Don't be afraid to experiment with new ideas and learn quickly from your

successes and failures. Agility and adaptability can be great competitive advantages in themselves.

5. **Build relationships and collaborations**: In the metaverse, companies can work together in new and exciting ways. Look for opportunities to collaborate with other companies, whether it's co-creating user experiences, integrating products and services, or reaching new audiences.

Remember that competitive advantages in the metaverse are not static, but evolve over time as the environment, technologies, and user needs and expectations change. Maintain an open and flexible approach, and be willing to re-evaluate and adjust your competitive advantages as your business and the metaverse develop.

2.8.4. Innovation and Specialization as Competitive Advantages

Innovation and specialization are two key strategies that companies can employ to gain a competitive advantage in the metaverse.

Innovation

Innovation refers to the introduction of new and improved ideas, processes or products. In the context of the metaverse, innovation can take many forms, from implementing emerging technologies to creating unique and engaging user experiences.

Innovation can help you stand out in a saturated market, attract and retain users, and stay ahead of your competitors.

The metaverse, with its immersive nature and interactivity, offers fertile ground for innovation. For example, you can innovate by creating new and exciting ways of interacting with your products or services, using virtual or augmented reality, or developing new forms of storytelling and brand building that take advantage of the potential of the metaverse.

Specialization

Specialization involves focusing on a specific market niche, or on a particular type of product or service, and seeking to be the best in that field. Specialization can enable you to more effectively meet the needs and desires of a particular group of users, and help you differentiate yourself from competitors who offer more generic products or services.

In the metaverse, specialization can take many forms. For example, you could specialize in creating immersive experiences for a specific target audience, such as music lovers, video game enthusiasts or fashion aficionados. Alternatively, you could focus on a particular type of metaverse experience, such as interactive adventures, learning experiences or live events.

Remember, the key to an effective competitive advantage is to offer unique and meaningful value to your target audience. Whether through innovation, specialization, or both, it is essential that you focus on what makes your business unique, and how you can use that to attract and retain users in the metaverse.

2.8.5. Collaboration and Operational Excellence as Competitive Advantages

Competitive advantages are not limited to innovation or specialization. In many cases, collaboration and operational excellence are two crucial strategies that can provide immense value in the context of the metaverse.

Collaboration

Collaboration refers to the ability to work together with other companies or individuals to achieve shared objectives. In the metaverse, this can happen through strategic partnerships, joint projects or the creation of engaged user communities.

Opportunities for collaboration in the metaverse are abundant and can range from partnerships with artists for the creation of unique NFTs, to alliances with other companies for the creation of combined multiversal spaces and experiences. By collaborating, companies can leverage each other's strengths and resources, achieving together what would be difficult or impossible to achieve independently.

Operational Excellence

Operational excellence refers to a company's ability to run its operations efficiently and effectively. In the metaverse, this may involve aspects such as optimizing content creation processes, effectively managing user relationships, or implementing state-of-the-art technologies and systems to ensure a smooth and seamless experience.

Operational excellence is critical to maintaining user satisfaction and loyalty in the metaverse. A company that can deliver high quality immersive experiences, without technical problems and with good customer service, will have a significant competitive advantage.

In summary, collaboration and operational excellence, as well as innovation and specialization, are valuable strategies that companies can use to develop a competitive advantage in the metaverse. By combining these strategies effectively, companies can differentiate themselves from their competitors and attract and retain users more effectively.

2.8.6. Leveraging Data to Create Competitive Advantages

Data is a critical source of competitive advantage in the metaverse. Every user interaction with the metaverse generates data that can be analyzed and used to improve the user experience, refine marketing strategies, develop more engaging products and services, and make more informed business decisions.

First, data can provide deep insights into users' preferences, behaviors and needs. This can enable companies to personalize their offerings and experiences, to better meet user expectations, and improve customer satisfaction and long-term loyalty.

In addition, data can help companies identify emerging trends and changes in user behavior, enabling them to adapt quickly to new market demands and opportunities. For example, data can reveal a growing interest in certain types of content, activities or social interactions, which can guide innovation and product development.

Data can also play a crucial role in improving operational efficiency and effectiveness. Companies can use data to optimize their content production processes, user management, customer support and other key operations, improving productivity and reducing costs.

Finally, the data can provide valuable insights into the performance of marketing and sales strategies, helping companies measure ROI and identify areas for improvement.

In short, strategically leveraging data can provide companies with a significant competitive advantage in the metaverse. However, it is important to remember that data collection and use must be carried out in an ethical manner that respects users' privacy and complies with all relevant regulations and standards.

2.8.7. Challenges and Considerations in the Development of Competitive Advantages in the Metaverse

In the search for competitive advantage in the metaverse, companies face a number of important challenges and considerations. Understanding and managing these factors is crucial to ensure successful and sustainable positioning in this emerging space.

One of the main challenges is the changing nature and evolution of the metaverse. Technologies, trends and user behaviors can change rapidly, and companies must be able to adapt with the same speed. This means keeping abreast of the latest developments, experimenting with new ideas and being willing to change course when necessary.

In addition, companies must be aware of the intense competition in the metaverse. With numerous companies and brands fighting for users' attention and loyalty, finding ways to stand out and offer unique value can be a very considerable challenge. This may require a deep understanding of the audience, a solid differentiation strategy and the ability to constantly innovate and surprise.

Developing an effective monetization strategy can also be a challenge. Companies must balance the need to generate revenue with the importance of delivering an engaging and satisfying user experience. This may involve exploring innovative monetization models, such as NFTs or micropayments, and creating mutual value opportunities for the company and users.

Finally, companies must consider the ethical and legal implications of their activities in the metaverse. This includes respecting the privacy and rights of users, responsible data management, and compliance with applicable regulations and standards.

In summary, while the metaverse offers great opportunities for developing competitive advantages, it also presents significant challenges, which companies must address diligently and strategically.

2.9. Key alliances

In today's hyper-connected economy, key partnerships have become an essential component of business growth and success. This reality is particularly evident in the metaverse, a constantly evolving digital environment that represents both exciting opportunities and significant challenges.

To enter and thrive in the metaverse, companies must recognize that this is not a territory that can be conquered in isolation. On the contrary, it is a space for collaboration and co-creation. The investment required to create a complete immersive environment, similar to platforms such as Decentraland, can be prohibitive for many organizations. In addition, building from scratch may not be the most efficient or effective strategy.

In this context, key alliances emerge as an essential strategic solution. These collaborations can enable companies to share costs, skills, technology and knowledge, allowing them to access the metaverse more efficiently and effectively.

In addition, partnerships can help companies access new audiences and markets, increase their visibility and reputation, and bring additional value to their offerings. They can also facilitate the exploration and adoption of new trends, technologies and business opportunities that arise in this dynamic environment.

Finally, in a world where user trust is increasingly important, partnerships with thought leaders and influencers in the metaverse can be a powerful way to foster audience engagement and loyalty.

However, forming and managing effective alliances is no simple task. It requires careful strategy, meticulous planning and execution, and effective relationship management.

2.9.1. Introduction to Key Alliances

Key alliances represent the formation of strategic links with other companies, organizations or individuals, with the objective of improving the positioning and performance of a business. These types of alliances can take various forms, from co-branding agreements to joint ventures, licensing, franchising, and participation in networks and business ecosystems.

In simple terms, key partnerships are collaborations that bring mutual value to all parties involved. For example, two companies could join together in a co-branding agreement to leverage their respective strengths and enhance their market position. A business could obtain a license to use another company's patented technology and thus increase its competitive advantage. Key alliances may even involve direct competitors, in what is known as "co-opetition", in which both parties collaborate in areas of mutual interest, while maintaining their competence in other areas.

In addition to improving market position, key alliances can provide numerous benefits, including expansion of market reach, acquisition of new competencies and capabilities, sharing of risks and benefits, and increased access to resources.

The importance of key alliances for the growth and success of a business is evident, and in the metaverse, this concept takes on even greater relevance. In this immersive and highly interconnected environment, key partnerships can unlock new opportunities and create synergies that drive the value and impact of a business in the metaverse.

2.9.2. Key Alliances in the Metaverse Context

In the metaverse, an immersive and dynamic digital environment, key partnerships take on a new dimension and value. The three-dimensional, interconnected digital spaces of the metaverse provide fertile ground for collaboration and co-creation. In it, companies and individuals can come together and work together in innovative and transformative ways, creating a new dimension of interaction and collaboration.

A key alliance in the metaverse may involve collaboration between brands to create joint immersive experiences. For example, a fashion company and a video game developer could team up to design and launch an exclusive line of virtual clothing within a game, creating a unique experience for users and generating mutual benefits for both brands.

Partnerships can also be with technology companies and metaverse platform providers. For example, a partnership with a virtual reality (VR) technology company could provide another company with the hardware or software needed to create immersive experiences in the metaverse. Similarly, a collaboration with a metaversal platform could give a company access to a new distribution channel and a large and engaged user base.

Finally, key partnerships may also include collaborations with influencers and content creators in the metaverse. These individuals may have a significant following in the metaverse and, therefore, could be valuable partners in increasing a brand's visibility and attracting new users.

2.9.3. Key Partnership Strategies for the Metaverse

Developing key alliances in the metaverse requires a well-designed and executed strategy. Below are some strategies that can be of great value when establishing partnerships in this environment:

1. **Identification of potential partners**: The first step is to identify potential partners whose interests and capabilities align with those of your company. These partners can range from technology companies and

metaverse platform developers to content creators and influencers with a presence in the metaverse.

2. **Complementarity assessment**: It is important to evaluate the complementarity between your company and potential partners. This may include complementarity of capabilities and resources, compatibility of target audiences and consistency of brand identities.

3. **Definition of shared objectives**: A key alliance in the metaverse must be based on shared objectives. These objectives can be as varied as developing new products or experiences, expanding reach and visibility, or improving competencies and capabilities.

4. **Establishment of terms and conditions**: Once the potential partners and shared objectives have been identified, it is necessary to define the terms and conditions of the alliance. This may include agreements on intellectual property, revenue sharing, and the roles and responsibilities of each partner.

5. **Creation of synergies**: The true value of a key alliance in the metaverse lies in the creation of synergies. This involves working together to create something that is greater than the sum of its parts, whether it's a unique immersive experience, a new virtual product or an innovative marketing campaign.

6. **Measurement and adjustment of results**: Finally, it is essential to measure the performance of the partnership and adjust the strategy based on the results. This involves

monitoring indicators such as user engagement, revenue generated and partner satisfaction.

In conclusion, a well-designed and executed key alliance strategy can give your company a competitive advantage in the metaverse, helping you innovate, differentiate and thrive in this dynamic and interconnected environment.

2.9.4. Impact of Key Alliances on the Value Proposition

Key partnerships can have a significant impact on the value proposition your company offers in the metaverse. Through partnerships, your business can strengthen and expand its value proposition in several ways:

1. **Enrichment of the offer**: An alliance with another entity can help complement and enhance your company's existing offering. This can mean the incorporation of new functionalities, services, products or experiences that align with users' needs and desires.

2. **Scope extension**: Partnerships can allow you to reach new user segments in the metaverse. This can translate into increased visibility and brand recognition, as well as new revenue opportunities.

3. **Access to new skills and technologies**: Through partnerships, your company can access new competencies, skills and technologies that would otherwise be difficult to acquire. This can improve the quality and innovation of your offer in the metaverse.

4. **Risk reduction**: Partnerships can also help share and minimize the risks associated with operating in the metaverse. This can be especially valuable in such a dynamic and constantly changing environment as the metaverse.

5. **Strengthening reputation and credibility**: Partnering with recognized and respected entities can strengthen your company's reputation and credibility in the metaverse. This can increase user trust and loyalty, thereby improving user engagement and retention.

6. **Sustainable development**: Partnerships can contribute to the sustainability and social responsibility of your company in the metaverse. For example, you could partner with organizations that promote inclusion, diversity, privacy, safety, security or environmental stewardship in the metaverse.

In short, key partnerships can provide your company with the tools and resources needed to offer a richer, more innovative and compelling value proposition in the metaverse. These alliances, if well managed, can be a strategic way to differentiate and gain a competitive advantage in this emerging environment.

2.9.5. Challenges and Considerations in Establishing Key Alliances in the Metaverse

Establishing key alliances in the metaverse, while it can provide multiple benefits, also comes with its own set of challenges and considerations. We explore some of the main areas to consider when developing these strategic partnerships:

1. **Compatibility and Alignment**: Not every company or entity will be a suitable potential partner for your business. It is crucial that there is compatibility in terms of corporate culture, values, objectives and expectations. Likewise, the value proposition of both parties must be aligned for the partnership to be mutually beneficial.

2. **Relationship Management**: Maintaining a healthy collaborative relationship can be challenging, as it requires effective communication, mutual respect, and the ability to resolve conflicts and disagreements constructively.

3. **Technical Integration**: The ability to effectively integrate the systems, platforms or technologies of both parties is a key aspect. This integration must be secure, efficient and capable of delivering a consistent and seamless user experience.

4. **Data Protection and Privacy**: In the metaverse, data protection and user privacy is an essential aspect to consider. Both parties must ensure that they adhere to the relevant regulations and standards, and that appropriate measures are taken to protect users' information and data.

5. **Legal and Contractual Framework**: The formulation of clear and comprehensive contractual agreements covering all aspects of the partnership is crucial. This may include aspects such as the responsibilities of each party,

profit sharing, intellectual property, and exit clauses, among others.

6. **Performance Evaluation and Measurement**: It is important to establish performance indicators and evaluation mechanisms to measure the effectiveness and success of the partnership. This information can help the parties make adjustments and improvements over time.

Finally, it is crucial to remember that key partnerships in the metaverse must be mutually beneficial, with each party bringing value to the other and to the end users. Through careful planning, effective management and thoughtful execution, your business can overcome these challenges and take full advantage of the opportunities that key partnerships in the metaverse can offer.

2.10. Cost structure

Understanding the cost structure of a company in the metaverse is vital to developing an effective business and marketing strategy. In the immersive metaverse environment, costs can be significantly different from a traditional business model, such as e-commerce or software as a service (SaaS). Rather than simply having to worry about the costs of web hosting, digital marketing and back-end operations, companies in the metaverse must also consider other additional and complex costs associated with creating and maintaining immersive environments and high-quality user experiences.

The computational burden required to operate in the metaverse is considerable, which can translate into significantly higher costs. This is due to the graphics- and data-intensive nature of these environments, which require high-level data processing and storage. This cost increases even more when considering the fact that users can interact with the environment in real time, which requires a high degree of performance and reliability.

For this reason it is essential to differentiate between the different types of costs, distinguishing between fixed and variable costs. Fixed costs, such as the infrastructure required to maintain the metaverse environment, may be high, but they do not change, regardless of the number of users or their level of activity. On the other hand, variable costs, such as the cost per user acquisition or the costs associated with the development and implementation of new features and experiences, can scale with business growth.

This analysis and understanding of the cost structure in the metaverse will enable companies to optimize their performance, improve their profitability and make informed strategic decisions. In the following subchapters, we will delve deeper into the nature of these costs and discuss strategies for their optimization and effective management. With this foundation, we can better understand how to create and maintain a successful and sustainable business in the metaverse.

2.10.1. Introduction to Cost Structure in the Metaverse

The cost structure represents one of the essential pillars in the design of any business model, and its relevance does not diminish when we talk about the metaverse. Before venturing into this new digital and immersive environment, it is critical to understand and plan for the investment required to operate and compete effectively.

In the metaverse, the cost structure takes on a new dimension, as it extends beyond the traditional costs associated with creating and managing a website or online store. The creation of immersive experiences, the development of digital assets or the management of user interaction and engagement are just a few examples of the new cost areas that companies must face.

As in any other business environment, in the metaverse there are fixed costs, which are those that the company must assume regardless of the volume of activity, and variable costs, which vary according to the activity and performance of the business.

Proper management and optimization of the cost structure in the metaverse can result in a more profitable and sustainable business. In turn, an efficient cost structure can enable companies to offer high-quality solutions and experiences at competitive prices, which can be a key factor in attracting and retaining users, as well as maintaining a competitive advantage in the metaverse.

2.10.2. Fixed and Variable Costs in the Metaverse

In the business world, costs are usually classified into two main categories: fixed costs and variable costs. In the metaverse, this classification remains valid, but the nature of these costs can vary in innovative and unique ways.

Fixed costs in the metaverse are those that must be paid, regardless of the activity or performance of your business. These costs are constant and do not change depending on the number of users or the level of interaction. Examples of fixed costs in the metaverse might include:

1. Development and maintenance of the technological infrastructure.
2. Hosting or hosting costs of the platform or virtual space.
3. Licenses and permissions for the use of specific software or technologies.
4. Salaries of the management and development team.

On the other hand, **variable costs** in the metaverse are those that change depending on the activity and performance of your business. These costs may increase or decrease depending on the number of users, the number of transactions and the amount of data processed, among other factors. Examples of variable costs in the metaverse might include:

1. Creation and updating of content and immersive experiences.
2. Marketing and advertising to attract and retain users.

3. Transaction costs and commissions for the sale of products or services.

4. Costs related to customer service and community management.

Proper management and analysis of fixed and variable costs will allow your business in the metaverse to maintain a financial balance, and ensure profitability and long-term sustainability. Furthermore, understanding and optimizing these costs is critical to establishing a competitive pricing strategy in this new and exciting digital environment.

2.10.3. Content and Technology Development and Maintenance

Content and technology development and maintenance represent two of the most significant costs in the metaverse. They are critical to ensure a quality immersive experience and to keep the business in line with changing user trends and expectations.

1. **Content Development**: Creating content for the metaverse is not a simple task. It goes beyond the creation of text, images or videos, as it requires the construction of environments, objects and interactive three-dimensional experiences that engage users. This may involve elements of virtual reality, augmented reality and video game development, all of which require a high degree of expertise and experience. Costs here may include designer and programmer salaries, design

and development software costs, and testing and tuning costs.

2. **Content Maintenance**: Once developed, content must be maintained and updated regularly to keep it relevant and attractive. This may involve adding new features, fixing bugs and problems, and adapting to new trends and user preferences. Content maintenance costs can vary considerably depending on the complexity and volume of the content.

3. **Technology Development**: The metaverse is based on advanced technologies that allow the creation of virtual spaces and real-time interaction. This may require the use of blockchain technologies for transactions and digital property, AI technologies for personalization and interaction, and VR and AR technologies for creating immersive experiences. Technology development costs can be substantial, including salaries for engineers and programmers, software licensing costs, and research and development costs.

4. **Technology Maintenance**: As with the content, the technology used in the metaverse needs constant maintenance and updating to ensure its optimal functioning and compatibility with current technological trends. This may involve technical support costs, upgrade and licensing costs, and security and data protection costs.

In summary, content and technology development and maintenance are critical aspects of the cost structure in the metaverse. Effective management of these costs is vital to ensure a high quality user experience, and to maintain business competitiveness in this dynamic and constantly evolving digital environment.

2.10.4. User Acquisition and Retention in the Metaverse

User acquisition and retention represent another crucial cost in the metaverse. Attracting users to your metaverse space and then keeping them engaged and active are critical to the success and sustainability of your business.

- **User Acquisition**: This cost refers to the activities and resources necessary to attract new users to your space in the metaverse. Acquisition methods can range from advertising campaigns and promotions, to creating engaging content and unique experiences that appeal to users. Strategic alliances with other players in the metaverse can also be effective in attracting new users. Acquisition costs can be high, depending on the competition, the nature of your proposition and the marketing tactics employed.

- **User Retention**: Once users have entered your metaverse space, it is important to keep them engaged and satisfied so that they stay. This involves providing an immersive and valuable experience, constantly updating and improving content and features, and listening and responding to user feedback and needs. User retention may also require the implementation of reward or loyalty systems, which may involve additional costs.

It is important to keep in mind that user acquisition and retention costs can vary considerably, depending on a number of factors, such as competition in the marketplace, the value and uniqueness of your offering, and the changing expectations and behaviors of users in the metaverse.

In addition, as metaverses continue to evolve and expand, the costs associated with user acquisition and retention are also likely to change and possibly increase. It is therefore vital for any business in the metaverse to have a clear understanding of these costs and be prepared to adapt and react as the metaverse environment evolves.

Ultimately, user acquisition and retention are critical to the success of any business in the metaverse, and require careful cost management and planning.

2.10.5. Channel Management and Promotion

Channel management and promotion are key components of any operation in the metaverse, and are therefore associated with their respective cost. Channel management refers to the organization and maintenance of the various channels or platforms through which you interact with your users, whether in the metaverse or in the real world. On the other hand, channel promotion refers to the strategies and tactics you implement to increase the visibility and attractiveness of your channels.

- **Channel Management**: Depending on the size and scope of your business in the metaverse, you may have several channels through which you interact with your users. These may include your metaverse space, a website, a social media platform, and a mobile app, among others. Managing these channels can involve significant costs, including developing and maintaining technology, moderating and responding to user comments and queries, regularly updating content and features, and monitoring and analyzing channel performance.

- **Channel Promotion**: Increasing the visibility and attractiveness of your channels is essential to attract and retain users. This can involve a variety of strategies and tactics, from advertising and marketing to public relations and strategic alliances. Channel promotion costs can vary widely, depending on the nature of your channels, your target audience, the competition in the marketplace and the tactics you choose to use.

It is important to keep in mind that channel management and promotion must be aligned with your overall business strategy and your goals in the metaverse. In addition, they should be monitored and evaluated regularly to ensure that they are providing a good return on investment and that they are effectively contributing to your goals and objectives.

2.10.6. Cost Structure Optimization in the Metaverse

In the metaverse, as in any other business space, it is essential to maintain rigorous control over the cost structure. However, the metaverse poses unique challenges and opportunities for cost optimization due to its immersive, interactive and technology-based nature. Below, we explore some strategies and approaches for cost structure optimization in the metaverse.

- **Automation and Digitalization**: Automation and digitization can be excellent tools to reduce costs in the metaverse. Processes such as content creation, user interaction, operations management and compliance can be automated or digitized to increase efficiency and reduce labor and administrative costs.

- **Efficient use of resources**: In the metaverse, resources such as time, space and energy can be used in highly efficient ways. For example, events and interactions can occur simultaneously at various locations and times, which can reduce logistics and travel costs. In addition, low-energy technologies and practices can be implemented to reduce energy costs.

- **Collaboration and Alliances**: Collaborations and alliances can be effective strategies for sharing and reducing costs in the metaverse. By working together with other players, you can share the costs of content and technology development and maintenance, user acquisition and retention, and channel management and promotion.

- **Adaptability and Continuous Learning**: In the metaverse, circumstances and user needs can change rapidly. By maintaining an attitude of adaptability and continuous learning, you can be more responsive to these changes and adjust your cost structure in a more effective and timely manner.

In summary, optimizing the cost structure in the metaverse requires a strategic, creative and flexible approach. By carefully balancing your costs and revenues, and continually looking for opportunities for improvement, you can increase the profitability and sustainability of your business in the metaverse.

3

METAVERSE CANVAS APPLICATION: SUCCESS STORIES

3.1. Fortnite and its transformation into the metaverse.

Fortnite, developed by Epic Games, started as a survival and building video game in 2017. However, over the years, it has evolved beyond its original purpose, becoming a space for social interaction, events and collaborations with brands and artists. Let's analyze how Fortnite uses the components of the Metaverse Canvas to achieve this success in the metaverse.

1. **Solution**: Fortnite has expanded its value proposition beyond a survival game, incorporating live events and immersive experiences, such as virtual concerts and movie releases.

2. **Target audience**: Fortnite has attracted a wide variety of gamers and non-gamers interested in social, entertainment and brand collaboration experiences, expanding its audience.

3. **Channels**: Fortnite uses its own gaming platform, Epic Games Store, to distribute and promote its events and experiences. It also uses social networks and content creators to reach new users.

4. **Immersive experience**: Fortnite live events, such as the Travis Scott and Marshmallow concerts, have delivered immersive experiences to millions of users simultaneously, with high quality visuals and sound.

5. **Sources of income**: Fortnite generates revenue through the sale of skins, items and battle passes, as well as through collaborations with brands and artists, who promote their products and services in the game.

6. **Key metrics**: Fortnite monitors metrics such as the number of active users, time spent in the game, and revenue generated from events and collaborations.

7. **NFT**: Although Fortnite has not yet incorporated NFT into its platform, there is great potential to introduce unique digital assets and collectibles in the future.

8. **Competitive advantage**: Fortnite has stood out in the video game market and the metaverse for its ability to innovate, adapt and offer unique and engaging experiences to its audience.

9. **Key alliances**: Fortnite has established partnerships with brands, artists and content creators, expanding its reach and strengthening its position in the metaverse.

10. **Cost structure**: Fortnite invests in developing and maintaining its platform, creating content and events, and promoting and acquiring users.

3.2. Decentraland and its blockchain-based virtual economy

Decentraland is a blockchain-based virtual reality platform where users can buy, sell and build virtual properties, as well as participate in immersive experiences and events. Let's see how Decentraland uses the components of the Metaverse Canvas to develop its business model in the metaverse.

1. **Solution**: Decentraland offers a decentralized metaverse, where users have control and ownership of their virtual assets, and can participate in a virtual economy based on cryptocurrencies.

2. **Target audience**: Decentraland targets users interested in virtual reality, blockchain technology and cryptocurrencies, as well as artists, developers and entrepreneurs looking for opportunities in the metaverse.

3. **Channels**: Decentraland uses its web platform and virtual reality applications to provide access to the metaverse, promoting its events and experiences through social media and collaborations with content creators.

4. **Immersive experience**: Decentraland users can explore and experience 3D virtual environments and events,

interact with other users and customize their avatars and properties.

5. **Sources of income**: Decentraland generates revenue through the sale of virtual land, commissions from transactions on its NFT marketplace and partnerships with companies and organizations that want to establish a presence in the metaverse.

6. **Key metrics**: Decentraland monitors metrics such as the number of active users, transactions made on its NFT marketplace and participation in virtual events and experiences.

7. **NFT**: NFTs play a central role in Decentraland's virtual economy, representing properties, objects and works of art that can be bought, sold and traded by users.

8. **Competitive advantage**: Decentraland is distinguished by its focus on decentralization, user ownership and control, and the integration of blockchain technology and cryptocurrencies into its metaverse.

9. **Key alliances**: Decentraland has established partnerships with blockchain technology companies, artists and content creators, as well as brands and organizations looking to explore opportunities in the metaverse.

10. **Cost structure**: Decentraland invests in the development and maintenance of its platform, the creation of content and virtual experiences, and the promotion and acquisition of users.

3.3. Roblox and its online gaming platform

Roblox is an online gaming platform that allows users to create and share their own games, and generate revenue by selling virtual goods and services. Let's look at how Roblox uses the components of the Metaverse Canvas to establish its business model in the metaverse.

1. **Solution**: Roblox provides a platform where developers and players can create, share and monetize virtual games and experiences of various genres and styles.

2. **Target audience**: Roblox targets a broad audience, including casual gamers, independent developers and companies looking to promote their brands and products in the metaverse.

3. **Channels**: Roblox uses its web platform, mobile and desktop applications to provide access to its games and experiences, promoting its content through social media, online advertising and collaborations with content creators.

4. **Immersive experience**: Roblox users can explore a wide variety of community-created virtual games and experiences, interact with other players and customize their avatars with virtual items.

5. **Sources of income**: Roblox generates revenue through the sale of its virtual currency, Robux, which users use to purchase items and services on the platform, and from commissions on sales made by developers.

6. **Key metrics**: Roblox monitors metrics such as the number of active users, transactions made on the platform, the number of games and experiences created and participation in virtual events.

7. **NFT**: Although Roblox has not yet integrated NFTs into its platform, there is great potential to incorporate unique and collectible digital assets in the future.

8. **Competitive advantage**: Roblox is distinguished by its focus on creativity and customization, allowing developers and players to create and share unique experiences on its platform.

9. **Key alliances**: Roblox has established partnerships with brands, artists and content creators looking to promote their products and services on the platform, as well as with technology and education companies that use Roblox to teach programming and design skills.

10. **Cost structure**: Roblox invests in the development and maintenance of its platform, the promotion and acquisition of users, and the support of the community of developers and content creators.

3.4. CryptoKitties and its blockchain-based crypto-pet marketplace

CryptoKitties is a blockchain-based game in which users can buy, sell, breed and collect unique virtual cats, represented as NFTs. Let's look at how CryptoKitties uses the components of the Metaverse Canvas to establish its business model in the metaverse.

1. **Solution**: CryptoKitties offers a blockchain-based crypto pet marketplace, where users can collect, breed and trade unique and rare virtual cats, represented as NFTs.

2. **Target audience**: CryptoKitties targets users interested in cryptocurrencies, blockchain technology and digital collectibles, as well as gaming enthusiasts and virtual pets.

3. **Channels**: CryptoKitties uses its web platform and mobile apps to provide access to its crypto pet marketplace, and promotes its content through social media, online advertising and collaborations with content creators.

4. **Immersive experience**: CryptoKitties users can explore the crypto pet market, interact with other collectors and participate in special events and promotions.

5. **Sources of income**: CryptoKitties generates revenue through the initial sale of virtual cats, transaction fees on its NFT marketplace and collaborations with artists and brands that create exclusive virtual cats.

6. **Key metrics**: CryptoKitties monitors metrics such as the number of active users, transactions made on its NFT marketplace and participation in events and promotions.

7. **NFT**: NFTs are central to CryptoKitties' business model, as they represent the scarcity and uniqueness of virtual cats, which users can collect and trade.

8. **Competitive advantage**: CryptoKitties is distinguished by its focus on blockchain technology and NFTs, offering a marketplace for digital collectibles based on scarcity and uniqueness.

9. **Key alliances**: CryptoKitties has established partnerships with artists, brands and content creators looking to promote their products and services through the creation of exclusive virtual cats.

10. **Cost structure**: CryptoKitties invests in the development and maintenance of its platform, the promotion and acquisition of users, and the creation of content and special events.

3.5. Somnium Space and its blockchain-based virtual reality platform

Somnium Space is a blockchain-based virtual reality metaverse where users can buy, sell and build virtual properties, as well as participate in immersive experiences and events. Let's see how Somnium Space uses the components of the Metaverse Canvas to develop its business model in the metaverse.

1. **Solution**: Somnium Space offers a virtual reality metaverse in which users have control and ownership of their virtual assets, and can participate in a virtual economy based on cryptocurrencies.

2. **Target audience**: Somnium Space focuses on users interested in virtual reality, blockchain technology and

cryptocurrencies, as well as artists, developers and entrepreneurs looking for opportunities in the metaverse.

3. **Channels**: Somnium Space uses its web platform and virtual reality applications to provide access to the metaverse, and promotes its events and experiences through social media and collaborations with content creators.

4. **Immersive experience**: Somnium Space users can explore and experience 3D virtual environments and events, interact with other users and customize their avatars and properties.

5. **Sources of income**: Somnium Space generates revenue through the sale of virtual land, commissions from transactions on its NFT marketplace and partnerships with companies and organizations that want to establish a presence in the metaverse.

6. **Key metrics**: Somnium Space monitors metrics such as the number of active users, transactions made on its NFT marketplace, and participation in virtual events and experiences.

7. **NFT**: NFTs play a central role in Somnium Space's virtual economy, representing property, objects and artwork that can be bought, sold and traded by users.

8. **Competitive advantage**: Somnium Space is distinguished by its focus on immersion and real-time interaction, offering a high-quality virtual reality experience, and the

integration of blockchain technology and cryptocurrencies into its metaverse.

9. **Key alliances**: Somnium Space has established partnerships with blockchain technology companies, artists and content creators, as well as brands and organizations looking to explore opportunities in the metaverse.

10. **Cost structure**: Somnium Space invests in the development and maintenance of its platform, the creation of content and virtual experiences, and the promotion and acquisition of users.

3.6. VRChat and its virtual reality social platform

VRChat is a virtual reality social platform where users can create and explore virtual worlds, interact with other users and participate in immersive events and experiences. Let's look at how VRChat uses the components of the Metaverse Canvas to establish its business model in the metaverse.

1. **Solution**: VRChat offers a virtual reality social platform that allows users to create and share virtual worlds and experiences, as well as interact with other users in real time.

2. **Target audience**: VRChat focuses on users interested in virtual reality and immersive experiences, including gamers, artists, developers and people looking to socialize in a virtual environment.

3. **Channels**: VRChat uses its web platform, virtual reality and desktop applications to provide access to its virtual worlds and experiences, and promotes its content through social media, collaborations with content creators and online events.

4. **Immersive experience**: VRChat users can explore a wide variety of community-created virtual worlds and experiences, interact with other users through personalized avatars, and participate in immersive events and activities.

5. **Sources of income**: VRChat generates revenue through its VRChat Plus subscription model, which offers subscribers additional benefits such as exclusive avatars and worlds, and through partnerships with companies and organizations looking to promote their products and services on the platform.

6. **Key metrics**: VRChat monitors metrics such as the number of active users, the number of worlds and experiences created, and participation in virtual events and activities.

7. **NFT**: Although VRChat has not yet integrated NFTs into its platform, there is great potential to incorporate unique and collectible digital assets in the future.

8. **Competitive advantage**: VRChat is distinguished by its focus on socialization and real-time interaction, offering an accessible and customizable virtual reality experience.

9. **Key alliances**: VRChat has established partnerships with artists, developers and content creators who create and

promote virtual experiences on the platform, as well as virtual reality hardware and technology companies.

10. **Cost structure**: VRChat invests in the development and maintenance of its platform, the promotion and acquisition of users, and the creation of content and virtual experiences.

3.7. Art Blocks and its NFT-based generative art platform

Art Blocks is a generative art platform that uses blockchain technology to create and sell unique works of art as NFTs. Let's look at how Art Blocks uses the components of the Metaverse Canvas to establish its business model in the metaverse.

1. **Solution**: Art Blocks offers an online platform that allows artists and creators to sell generative artwork as NFT, and collectors to acquire and market these unique pieces.

2. **Target audience**: Art Blocks focuses on artists and creators interested in generative art and cryptocurrencies, as well as collectors and digital art enthusiasts.

3. **Channels**: Art Blocks uses its web platform and mobile applications to provide access to its generative art marketplace, and promotes its content through social media, online advertising and collaborations with content creators.

4. **Immersive experience**: Art Blocks users can explore the generative art market, interact with other collectors and artists, and participate in special events and promotions.

5. **Sources of income**: Art Blocks generates revenue through the initial sale of generative artwork, commissions from transactions on its NFT marketplace, and collaborations with artists and brands that create exclusive artwork.

6. **Key metrics**: Art Blocks monitors metrics such as the number of active users, transactions made on its NFT marketplace, and participation in events and promotions.

7. **NFT**: NFTs are central to the Art Blocks business model, as they represent the uniqueness and authenticity of generative artworks that users can collect and trade.

8. **Competitive advantage**: Art Blocks is distinguished by its focus on generative art and blockchain technology, offering a digital collectibles marketplace based on uniqueness and authenticity.

9. **Key alliances**: Art Blocks has established partnerships with artists, brands and content creators looking to promote their products and services through the creation of exclusive generative artwork.

10. **Cost structure**: Art Blocks invests in the development and maintenance of its platform, the promotion and acquisition of users, and the creation of content and special events.

3.8. Horizon Workrooms and its virtual reality collaboration platform

Horizon Workrooms is a virtual reality collaboration platform developed by Meta (formerly Facebook), designed to facilitate meetings and teamwork in immersive virtual environments. Let's see how Horizon Workrooms uses the components of the Metaverse Canvas to establish its business model in the metaverse.

1. **Solution**: Horizon Workrooms offers a virtual reality collaboration platform that enables users to participate in meetings, events and teamwork sessions in three-dimensional, interactive virtual environments.

2. **Target audience**: Horizon Workrooms focuses on professionals, businesses and organizations looking for more immersive and effective online collaboration solutions.

3. **Channels**: Horizon Workrooms uses its web platform and virtual reality applications to provide access to its virtual collaboration environments, and promotes its services through online advertising, social media and partnerships with companies and organizations.

4. **Immersive experience**: Horizon Workrooms users can participate in meetings and teamwork sessions in virtual environments that simulate physical spaces, interact with other users and share content in real time.

5. **Sources of income**: Horizon Workrooms generates revenue through subscriptions and licenses for companies and organizations using the virtual reality collaboration platform.

6. **Key metrics**: Horizon Workrooms monitors metrics such as the number of active users, the number of meetings and teamwork sessions held, and user satisfaction with the platform.

7. **NFT**: Although Horizon Workrooms is not focused on NFT, there is potential to incorporate unique and collectible digital assets in the future, such as design objects to customize virtual work environments.

8. **Competitive advantage**: Horizon Workrooms is distinguished by its focus on virtual reality collaboration and integration with other Meta services and tools, offering an immersive and effective teamwork experience.

9. **Key alliances**: Horizon Workrooms has established partnerships with companies and organizations seeking online collaboration solutions, as well as virtual reality hardware manufacturers and related service providers.

10. **Cost structure**: Horizon Workrooms invests in the development and maintenance of its platform, the promotion and acquisition of users and the integration with other Meta services and tools.

4

APPLICATION OF THE METAVERSE CANVAS: MARKETING ACTIONS IN THE METAVERSE

4.1. Nike and its collaboration with Roblox in the metaverse

Nike, the famous sports footwear and apparel brand, has collaborated with Roblox, a popular online entertainment platform, to create immersive experiences and promote its products in the metaverse. Let's take a look at how Nike has leveraged the Metaverse Canvas components in this collaboration.

1. **Solution**: Nike has developed immersive and personalized experiences within Roblox, allowing users to interact with the brand and its products in a virtual environment.

2. **Target audience**: The collaboration between Nike and Roblox is aimed at a young and active audience interested in fashion, sports and online entertainment.

3. **Channels**: Nike uses the Roblox platform to present its immersive experiences and promote the collaboration through social media, online advertising and live events.

4. **Immersive experience**: Users can explore Nike-themed virtual spaces, interact with other users, test and purchase Nike products, and participate in exclusive events and challenges.

5. **Sources of income**: Nike generates revenue through the sale of virtual products and accessories within Roblox, as well as through increased brand awareness and cross-promotion of its physical products.

6. **Key metrics**: Nike monitors metrics such as the number of users interacting with their Roblox experiences, virtual product sales, and the impact on brand awareness and physical product sales.

7. **NFT**: While this collaboration is not focused on NFT, there is potential to incorporate unique and collectible digital assets in the future, such as limited edition footwear and virtual sportswear.

8. **Competitive advantage**: Nike distinguishes itself in this collaboration through its ability to create immersive and personalized experiences in Roblox, encouraging interaction with the brand and its products in a virtual environment.

9. **Key alliances**: The collaboration with Roblox is critical to the success of Nike's initiative in the metaverse, allowing

the brand to leverage the platform's popularity and its young, engaged audience.

10. **Cost structure**: Nike invests in the development of virtual experiences, the promotion and acquisition of users and the creation of exclusive content and events in Roblox.

4.2. Gucci and its collaboration with Roblox in the metaverse

Gucci, the renowned Italian luxury brand, has collaborated with Roblox, the aforementioned popular online entertainment platform, to present immersive experiences and promote its products in the metaverse. Let's take a look at how Gucci has leveraged the components of the Metaverse Canvas in this collaboration.

1. **Solution**: Gucci has developed immersive and exclusive experiences within Roblox, allowing users to interact with the brand and its products in a virtual environment.

2. **Target audience**: The collaboration between Gucci and Roblox is aimed at a young and sophisticated audience interested in fashion, luxury and online entertainment.

3. **Channels**: Gucci uses the Roblox platform to present its immersive experiences and promote the collaboration through social media, online advertising and exclusive events.

4. **Immersive experience**: Users can explore Gucci-themed virtual spaces, interact with other users, try and buy Gucci products and participate in brand events and challenges.

5. **Sources of income**: Gucci generates revenue through the sale of virtual products and accessories within Roblox, as well as through increased brand awareness and cross-promotion of its physical products.

6. **Key metrics**: Gucci monitors metrics such as the number of users interacting with their Roblox experiences, virtual product sales and the impact on brand awareness and physical product sales.

7. **NFT**: While this collaboration is not focused on NFT, there is potential to incorporate unique and collectible digital assets in the future, such as limited edition virtual luxury apparel and accessories.

8. **Competitive advantage**: Gucci stands out in this collaboration for its ability to create immersive and exclusive experiences in Roblox, fostering interaction with the brand and its products in a luxury virtual environment.

9. **Key alliances**: The collaboration with Roblox is critical to the success of Gucci's initiative in the metaverse, as it allows the brand to leverage the platform's popularity and its young, engaged audience.

10. **Cost structure**: Gucci invests in the development of virtual experiences, the promotion and acquisition of

users, and the creation of exclusive content and events on Roblox.

4.3. Balenciaga and its collaboration with Fortnite in the metaverse.

Balenciaga, the prestigious luxury fashion brand, has collaborated with Fortnite, a popular video game and online entertainment platform, to present immersive experiences and promote its products in the metaverse. Let's take a look at how Balenciaga has leveraged the Metaverse Canvas components in this collaboration.

1. **Solution**: Balenciaga has developed virtual fashion collections and immersive experiences within Fortnite, allowing users to interact with the brand and its products in a virtual environment.

2. **Target audience**: The collaboration between Balenciaga and Fortnite is aimed at a young and sophisticated audience interested in fashion, luxury and online entertainment.

3. **Channels**: Balenciaga uses the Fortnite platform to present its virtual fashion collections and promote the collaboration through social media, online advertising and exclusive events.

4. **Immersive experience**: Users can purchase and wear Balenciaga garments on their in-game avatars, interact

with other users and participate in brand events and challenges.

5. **Sources of income**: Balenciaga generates revenue through the sale of virtual products and accessories within Fortnite, as well as through increased brand awareness and cross-promotion of its physical products.

6. **Key metrics**: Balenciaga monitors metrics such as the number of users interacting with their Fortnite experiences, virtual product sales, and the impact on brand perception and physical product sales.

7. **NFT**: While this collaboration is not focused on NFT, there is potential to incorporate unique and collectible digital assets in the future, such as limited edition virtual luxury apparel and accessories.

8. **Competitive advantage**: Balenciaga stands out in this collaboration for its ability to create virtual fashion collections and immersive experiences in Fortnite, fostering interaction with the brand and its products in a luxury virtual environment.

9. **Key alliances**: The collaboration with Fortnite is critical to the success of Balenciaga's initiative in the metaverse, allowing the brand to leverage the platform's popularity and its young, engaged audience.

10. **Cost structure**: Balenciaga invests in the development of virtual fashion collections, user promotion and acquisition, and the creation of exclusive content and events for Fortnite.

4.4. Louis Vuitton and its partnership with League of Legends in the metaverse

Louis Vuitton, the iconic French luxury brand, has collaborated with League of Legends, a popular video game and online entertainment platform, to present immersive experiences and promote its products in the metaverse. Let's take a look at how Louis Vuitton has leveraged the components of the Metaverse Canvas in this collaboration.

1. **Solution**: Louis Vuitton has developed virtual fashion collections and immersive experiences within League of Legends, allowing users to interact with the brand and its products in a virtual environment.

2. **Target audience**: The collaboration between Louis Vuitton and League of Legends is aimed at a young and sophisticated audience interested in fashion, luxury and online entertainment.

3. **Channels**: Louis Vuitton uses the League of Legends platform to present its virtual fashion collections and promote the collaboration through social media, online advertising and exclusive events.

4. **Immersive experience**: Users can purchase and wear Louis Vuitton garments on their in-game avatars, interact with other users and participate in brand events and challenges.

5. **Sources of income**: Louis Vuitton generates revenue through the sale of virtual products and accessories

within League of Legends, as well as through increased brand awareness and cross-promotion of its physical products.

6. **Key metrics**: Louis Vuitton monitors metrics such as the number of users interacting with their League of Legends experiences, virtual product sales and the impact on brand perception and physical product sales.

7. **NFT**: While this collaboration is not focused on NFT, there is potential to incorporate unique and collectible digital assets in the future, such as limited edition virtual luxury apparel and accessories.

8. **Competitive advantage**: Louis Vuitton distinguishes itself in this collaboration through its ability to create virtual fashion collections and immersive experiences in League of Legends, fostering interaction with the brand and its products in a luxury virtual environment.

9. **Key alliances**: The partnership with League of Legends is critical to the success of Louis Vuitton's initiative in the metaverse, allowing the brand to leverage the platform's popularity and its young, engaged audience.

10. **Cost structure**: Louis Vuitton invests in the development of virtual fashion collections, the promotion and acquisition of users, and the creation of exclusive content and events in League of Legends.

4.5. Coca-Cola and its collaboration with Decentraland in the Metaverse

Coca-Cola, the world-renowned beverage brand, has collaborated with Decentraland, a blockchain-based metaverse platform, to present immersive experiences and promote its products in the metaverse. Let's take a look at how Coca-Cola has leveraged the components of the Metaverse Canvas in this collaboration.

1. **Solution**: Coca-Cola has developed immersive experiences and virtual spaces within Decentraland, allowing users to interact with the brand and its products in a virtual environment.

2. **Target audience**: The collaboration between Coca-Cola and Decentraland is aimed at a broad audience interested in beverages, online entertainment and digital experiences.

3. **Channels**: Coca-Cola uses Decentraland's platform to present its immersive experiences and virtual spaces, and promote collaboration through social networks, online advertising and exclusive events.

4. **Immersive experience**: Users can explore virtual Coca-Cola spaces, interact with brand avatars and participate in Coca-Cola events and challenges in Decentraland.

5. **Sources of income**: Coca-Cola generates revenue through increased brand awareness and cross-promotion

of its products, both in the metaverse and in the physical world.

6. **Key metrics**: Coca-Cola monitors metrics such as the number of users interacting with its Decentraland experiences, the impact on brand perception and sales of its products.

7. **NFT**: Coca-Cola has created collectible and exclusive NFTs, such as limited editions of its virtual products and accessories, which can be purchased and traded by users on Decentraland.

8. **Competitive advantage**: Coca-Cola stands out in this collaboration for its ability to create immersive experiences and virtual spaces in Decentraland, encouraging interaction with the brand and its products in a dynamic virtual environment.

9. **Key alliances**: The partnership with Decentraland is critical to the success of Coca-Cola's metaverse initiative, allowing the brand to leverage the popularity of the platform and its audience interested in digital experiences.

10. **Cost structure**: Coca-Cola invests in the development of virtual experiences, the promotion and acquisition of users, and the creation of exclusive content and events in Decentraland.

4.6. Warner Bros. and its collaboration with The Sandbox in the metaverse

Warner Bros, the well-known film and entertainment studio, has collaborated with The Sandbox, a blockchain-based metaverse platform, to present immersive experiences and promote its intellectual properties in the metaverse. Let's take a look at how Warner Bros. has leveraged the components of the Metaverse Canvas in this collaboration.

1. **Solution**: Warner Bros. has developed immersive experiences and virtual spaces within The Sandbox, allowing users to interact with the brand's intellectual properties in a virtual environment.

2. **Target audience**: The collaboration between Warner Bros. and The Sandbox is aimed at an audience interested in movies, series, online entertainment and digital experiences.

3. **Channels**: Warner Bros. uses The Sandbox platform to present its immersive experiences and virtual spaces, and promote the collaboration through social media, online advertising and exclusive events.

4. **Immersive experience**: Users can explore virtual spaces based on Warner Bros. intellectual properties, interact with characters and participate in events and challenges in The Sandbox.

5. **Sources of income**: Warner Bros. generates revenue through increased awareness of its intellectual properties

and cross-promotion of its products, both in the metaverse and in the physical world.

6. **Key metrics**: Warner Bros monitors metrics such as the number of users interacting with their experiences in The Sandbox, the impact on the perception of their intellectual properties and sales of related products.

7. **NFT**: Warner Bros. has created collectible and exclusive NFTs, such as limited editions of its products, virtual accessories and characters based on its intellectual properties, which can be purchased and traded by users in The Sandbox.

8. **Competitive advantage**: Warner Bros. distinguishes itself in this collaboration through its ability to create immersive experiences and virtual spaces in The Sandbox, encouraging interaction with its intellectual properties in an engaging virtual environment.

9. **Key alliances**: The collaboration with The Sandbox is critical to the success of Warner Bros.' initiative in the metaverse, allowing the brand to leverage the popularity of the platform and its audience interested in digital entertainment and experiences.

10. **Cost structure**: Warner Bros. invests in the development of virtual experiences, the promotion and acquisition of users, and the creation of exclusive content and events in The Sandbox.

4.7. Calvin Klein and his collaboration with Animal Crossing in the Metaverse

Calvin Klein, the prestigious fashion and clothing brand, has collaborated with Animal Crossing: New Horizons, the popular social simulation video game developed by Nintendo, to present immersive experiences and promote its products in the metaverse. Let's take a look at how Calvin Klein has leveraged the components of the Metaverse Canvas in this collaboration.

1. **Solution**: Calvin Klein has developed virtual clothing and accessories within Animal Crossing: New Horizons, allowing users to dress their characters with the brand's products in a virtual environment.

2. **Target audience**: The collaboration between Calvin Klein and Animal Crossing is aimed at an audience interested in fashion, lifestyle and digital experiences in video games.

3. **Channels**: Calvin Klein uses the Animal Crossing video game: New Horizons to present its virtual products and promote the collaboration through social media, online advertising and exclusive events.

4. **Immersive experience**: Users can customize their characters in Animal Crossing with Calvin Klein clothing and accessories, creating an emotional bond with the brand and its products in a virtual environment.

5. **Sources of income**: Calvin Klein generates revenue through increased brand awareness and cross-promotion

of its products, both in the metaverse and in the physical world.

6. **Key metrics**: Calvin Klein monitors metrics such as the number of users interacting with its products on Animal Crossing, the impact on brand perception and sales of its products.

7. **NFT**: Although Animal Crossing does not use blockchain technology, Calvin Klein can create exclusive in-game virtual products to encourage interaction with the brand and increase its visibility in the metaverse.

8. **Competitive advantage**: Calvin Klein distinguishes itself in this collaboration for its ability to create attractive and quality virtual products in Animal Crossing, encouraging interaction with the brand and its products in a personalized virtual environment.

9. **Key alliances**: Collaboration with Animal Crossing: New Horizons is critical to the success of Calvin Klein's metaverse initiative, allowing the brand to leverage the popularity of the video game and its audience interested in fashion and digital experiences.

10. **Cost structure**: Calvin Klein invests in virtual product development, user promotion and acquisition, and the creation of exclusive Animal Crossing content and events.

5

INVENTED CAMPAIGN PROPOSALS

5.1. L'Oréal and its partnership with VRChat in the metaverse

L'Oréal, the renowned beauty and cosmetics brand, has collaborated with VRChat, a virtual chat and metaverse platform, to present a virtual beauty experience in the metaverse. Let's take a look at how L'Oréal has leveraged the components of the Metaverse Canvas in this collaboration.

1. **Solution**: L'Oréal has developed a virtual space on VRChat, which allows users to try on and purchase virtual makeup products in real time, offering a unique and immersive beauty experience.

2. **Target audience**: The collaboration between L'Oréal and VRChat is aimed at an audience interested in beauty, fashion and digital experiences.

3. **Channels**: L'Oréal uses the VRChat platform to present its virtual beauty experience and promote the collaboration through social media, online advertising and exclusive events.

4. **Immersive experience**: Users can explore and enjoy L'Oréal's virtual space on VRChat, interacting with virtual makeup products and creating customized looks in real time.

5. **Sources of income**: L'Oréal generates revenue through increased brand awareness and the sale of virtual makeup products in the metaverse.

6. **Key metrics**: L'Oréal monitors metrics such as the number of users interacting with its virtual beauty experience on VRChat, the impact on brand awareness and sales of its products.

7. **NFT**: L'Oréal uses NFT to offer exclusive and customizable virtual makeup products to users, allowing shoppers to prove the authenticity and ownership of their purchases in the metaverse.

8. **Competitive advantage**: L'Oreal distinguishes itself in this partnership through its ability to create an engaging and innovative virtual beauty experience on VRChat, encouraging interaction with the brand and its products in a personalized virtual environment.

9. **Key alliances**: The partnership with VRChat is critical to the success of L'Oréal's metaverse initiative, allowing the brand to leverage the platform's popularity and its audience interested in digital experiences.

10. **Cost structure**: L'Oréal invests in developing its virtual beauty experience, promoting and acquiring users, and creating exclusive content and events on VRChat.

5.2. Adidas and its collaboration with Decentraland in the metaverse

Adidas, the renowned athletic apparel and footwear brand, has collaborated with Decentraland, a blockchain-based metaverse platform, to introduce an exclusive line of virtual apparel in the metaverse. Let's see how Adidas has used the Metaverse Canvas components in this collaboration:

1. **Solution**: Adidas has created a collection of exclusive virtual clothing and accessories for the metaverse, offering Decentraland users the possibility to customize their avatars with Adidas products.

2. **Target audience**: The collaboration between Adidas and Decentraland is aimed at a young audience interested in fashion, sports and digital experiences, as well as blockchain technology enthusiasts.

3. **Channels**: Adidas uses the Decentraland platform to present its virtual collection and promote the collaboration through social media, online advertising and exclusive events within the metaverse.

4. **Immersive experience**: Users can explore and enjoy the Adidas virtual space in Decentraland, interacting with Adidas products and customizing their avatars with virtual clothing and accessories.

5. **Sources of income**: Adidas generates revenue through the sale of its exclusive virtual products and increased brand awareness in the metaverse.

6. **Key metrics**: Adidas monitors metrics such as the number of users interacting with its virtual space on Decentraland, the impact on brand perception and sales of its virtual products.

7. **NFT**: Adidas uses NFT to offer exclusive and authentic virtual products to users, allowing shoppers to prove the authenticity and ownership of their purchases in the metaverse.

8. **Competitive advantage**: Adidas distinguishes itself in this collaboration through its ability to create an engaging and innovative virtual fashion experience on Decentraland, encouraging interaction with the brand and its products in a personalized virtual environment.

9. **Key alliances**: The partnership with Decentraland is critical to the success of Adidas' metaverse initiative, allowing the brand to leverage the platform's popularity, its blockchain technology and its audience interested in digital experiences.

10. **Cost structure**: Adidas invests in the development of its virtual collection, the promotion and acquisition of users, and the creation of exclusive content and events on Decentraland.

5.3. Swarovski and its collaboration with Spatial.io in the metaverse

Swarovski, the prestigious jewelry and accessories brand, has collaborated with Spatial.io, a virtual reality and metaverse platform, to present a jewelry shopping experience in the metaverse. Let's take a look at how Swarovski has used the Metaverse Canvas components in this collaboration:

1. **Solution**: Swarovski has developed a virtual space on Spatial.io that allows users to explore, try on and purchase the brand's jewelry products in real time, offering a unique and immersive shopping experience.

2. **Target audience**: The collaboration between Swarovski and Spatial.io is aimed at an audience interested in jewelry, fashion and digital experiences.

3. **Channels**: Swarovski uses the Spatial.io platform to present its virtual shopping experience and promote the collaboration through social media, online advertising and exclusive events.

4. **Immersive experience**: Users can explore and enjoy Swarovski's virtual space on Spatial.io, interacting with jewelry products and experiencing a personalized shopping experience.

5. **Sources of income**: Swarovski generates revenue through increased brand awareness and sales of jewelry products in the metaverse.

6. **Key metrics**: Swarovski monitors metrics such as the number of users interacting with their virtual shopping experience on Spatial.io, the impact on brand awareness and sales of its products.

7. **NFT**: Swarovski uses NFT to offer exclusive and customizable virtual jewelry products to users, allowing buyers to prove the authenticity and ownership of their purchases in the metaverse.

8. **Competitive advantage**: Swarovski distinguishes itself in this collaboration through its ability to create an engaging and innovative virtual shopping experience on Spatial.io, encouraging interaction with the brand and its products in a personalized virtual environment.

9. **Key alliances**: The collaboration with Spatial.io is critical to the success of Swarovski's metaverse initiative, allowing the brand to leverage the platform's popularity and its audience interested in digital experiences.

10. **Cost structure**: Swarovski invests in developing its virtual shopping experience, promoting and acquiring users, and creating exclusive content and events on Spatial.io.

5.4. Marriott International and its collaboration with VRChat in the Metaverse

Marriott International, the renowned hotel and lodging chain, has collaborated with VRChat, a virtual chat platform in the metaverse, to present immersive experiences and promote its services in the metaverse. Let's take a look at how Marriott International has leveraged the components of the Metaverse Canvas in this collaboration.

1. **Solution**: Marriott International has developed virtual spaces that replicate its hotels and accommodations within VRChat, allowing users to experience the brand's services and environments in a virtual setting.

2. **Target audience**: The collaboration between Marriott International and VRChat is aimed at an audience interested in travel, hospitality and digital experiences.

3. **Channels**: Marriott International uses the VRChat platform to present its virtual spaces and promote collaboration through social networks, online advertising and exclusive events.

4. **Immersive experience**: Users can explore and enjoy Marriott International's virtual spaces in VRChat, creating an emotional bond with the brand and its services in a virtual environment.

5. **Sources of income**: Marriott International generates revenue through increased brand awareness and cross-promotion of its services, both in the metaverse and in the physical world.

6. **Key metrics**: Marriott International monitors metrics such as the number of users interacting with its virtual spaces on VRChat, the impact on brand awareness and bookings of its hotels and accommodations.

7. **NFT**: Although VRChat does not use blockchain technology, Marriott International can create unique and personalized virtual experiences for its customers on the platform.

8. **Competitive advantage**: Marriott International distinguishes itself in this collaboration for its ability to create attractive and quality virtual spaces in VRChat, encouraging interaction with the brand and its services in a personalized virtual environment.

9. **Key alliances**: The partnership with VRChat is critical to the success of Marriott International's metaverse initiative, allowing the brand to leverage the platform's popularity and its audience interested in digital experiences.

10. **Cost structure**: Marriott International invests in the development of virtual spaces, the promotion and acquisition of users, and the creation of exclusive content and events in VRChat.

5.5. American Eagle and its collaboration with Genies in the Metaverse

American Eagle, the well-known fashion and apparel brand, has collaborated with Genies, a digital avatar platform in the metaverse, to present immersive experiences and promote its products in the metaverse. Let's take a look at how American Eagle has leveraged the components of the Metaverse Canvas in this collaboration.

1. **Solution**: American Eagle has developed virtual clothing and accessories within Genies, allowing users to dress their avatars with the brand's products in a virtual environment.

2. **Target audience**: The collaboration between American Eagle and Genies targets an audience interested in fashion, lifestyle and digital experiences.

3. **Channels**: American Eagle uses the Genies platform to showcase its virtual products and promote the collaboration through social media, online advertising and exclusive events.

4. **Immersive experience**: Users can customize their avatars in Genies with American Eagle apparel and accessories, creating an emotional bond with the brand and its products in a virtual environment.

5. **Sources of income**: American Eagle generates revenue through increased brand awareness and cross-promotion of its products, both in the metaverse and in the physical world.

6. **Key metrics**: American Eagle monitors metrics such as the number of users interacting with its products on Genies, the impact on brand awareness and sales of its products.

7. **NFT**: American Eagle has created collectible and exclusive NFTs, such as limited editions of its virtual products and accessories, which can be purchased and traded by users on Genies.

8. **Competitive advantage**: American Eagle distinguishes itself in this partnership through its ability to create engaging and quality virtual products in Genies,

encouraging interaction with the brand and its products in a personalized virtual environment.

9. **Key alliances**: The partnership with Genies is critical to the success of American Eagle's metaverse initiative, allowing the brand to leverage the platform's popularity and its audience interested in fashion and digital experiences.

10. **Cost structure**: American Eagle invests in virtual product development, promotion and user acquisition, and the creation of exclusive content and events in Genies.

5.6. BMW and its collaboration with Somnium Space in the Metaverse

BMW, the renowned German automaker, has collaborated with Somnium Space, a virtual reality and metaverse platform, to present immersive experiences and promote its vehicles in the metaverse. Let's take a look at how BMW has leveraged the components of the Metaverse Canvas in this collaboration.

1. **Solution**: BMW has developed immersive experiences and virtual showrooms within Somnium Space, allowing users to interact with the brand and its vehicles in a virtual environment.

2. **Target audience**: The collaboration between BMW and Somnium Space is aimed at an audience interested in high quality automobiles, technology and online entertainment.

3. **Channels**: BMW uses the Somnium Space platform to present its immersive experiences and virtual showrooms, and promote the collaboration through social media, online advertising and exclusive events.

4. **Immersive experience**: Users can explore virtual BMW showrooms, interact with BMW vehicles and avatars, and participate in BMW events and challenges in Somnium Space.

5. **Sources of income**: BMW generates revenue through increased brand awareness and cross-promotion of its vehicles, both in the metaverse and in the physical world.

6. **Key metrics**: BMW monitors metrics such as the number of users interacting with their Somnium Space experiences, the impact on brand perception and vehicle sales.

7. **NFT**: While this collaboration is not focused on NFT, there is potential to incorporate unique and collectible digital assets in the future, such as limited edition vehicles and virtual accessories.

8. **Competitive advantage**: BMW stands out in this collaboration for its ability to create immersive experiences and virtual showrooms in Somnium Space, encouraging interaction with the brand and its products in a high quality virtual environment.

9. **Key alliances**: The collaboration with Somnium Space is critical to the success of BMW's initiative in the metaverse, allowing the brand to leverage the platform's

popularity and its audience interested in technology and automobiles.

10. **Cost structure**: BMW invests in the development of virtual experiences, the promotion and acquisition of users, and the creation of exclusive content and events in Somnium Space.

6

IDEAS AND INSPIRATIONS FOR BRANDS IN THE METAVERSE

6.1. IKEA: Virtual Interior Design and Decoration

IKEA could become active in the metaverse to bring its interior design and decoration value proposition to the virtual environment. The company could create a metaverse experience in which users could design and decorate their own virtual spaces using IKEA products. This project would not only increase the visibility and reach of the brand, but also provide a new platform for commerce and product experimentation. The objective of this project would be to extend its brand and products to new environments, increasing its interaction with customers and providing a new channel for sales.

Metaverse Canvas: IKEA

1. **Solution**: IKEA offers an interior design and decoration platform in the metaverse, where users can experience the brand's products in an immersive, three-dimensional environment.

2. **Target audience**: The target audience for this solution is mainly consumers of furniture and decorative products, especially those with an interest in interior design and home decoration. This audience would greatly benefit from being able to view products in their own space before purchasing them.

3. **Channels**: The main channels would be the IKEA metaverse platform and the IKEA online store, where users could buy the selected products in their virtual design.

4. **Immersive experience**: In addition to visualizing IKEA products in their own spaces, users could interact with the platform to customize products, change colors, textures and sizes in real time, providing a highly personalized and detailed interior design experience. Another experience could be the ability to explore homes decorated by famous interior designers or decorating influencers, providing inspiration and new ideas for your own space.

5. **Sources of income**: In addition to product sales, IKEA could explore additional forms of monetization through NFTs. For example, they could create exclusive "Interior Design" NFTs, allowing users to purchase and own unique designs for their virtual spaces. These NFT interior designs could be created in collaboration with renowned interior designers, adding value and exclusivity to them.

6. **Key metrics**: Key metrics could include the number of active users on the platform, number of designs created, design-to-purchase conversion rate and customer satisfaction.

7. **NFT**: In addition to the "Interior Designs" NFT, IKEA could also explore the creation of NFT for its own products. Users could then buy, own and sell IKEA products in NFT format on the metaverse platform, adding an additional layer of ownership and interactivity to their experience.

8. **Competitive advantage**: IKEA has a strong competitive advantage thanks to being a recognized brand and its wide range of affordable designer products. Its entry into the metaverse would allow it to offer a unique and immersive user experience.

9. **Key alliances**: In the metaverse, IKEA could consider partnerships with metaverse platforms such as Decentraland or Crypto Voxels, which have large user communities and experience in creating immersive environments. They could also explore collaborations with technology brands such as Oculus to leverage virtual reality capabilities, or with interior design software companies such as SketchUp or AutoCAD to integrate more advanced design tools into their platform.

10. **Cost structure**: Costs associated with this project would include the development and maintenance of the metaverse platform, logistics and product delivery

costs, and any costs associated with partnering and collaborating with interior designers and other partners.

6.2. Tesla: Virtual Driving Test

Tesla could leverage the metaverse to offer virtual test drive experiences. Users would be able to experience driving a Tesla in different environments and conditions, providing them with an immersive and interactive user experience that could increase brand awareness and interest in its products. The objective of this action would be to provide a unique user experience, realistically showcasing the features and benefits of its vehicles.

Metaverse Canvas: Tesla

1. **Solution**: Tesla could create an immersive virtual test drive experience, where users could experience driving a Tesla in a variety of environments and conditions. This experience would provide users with a deeper and more realistic understanding of what it feels like to drive a Tesla, and at the same time, allow Tesla to demonstrate the superior capabilities of its vehicles.

2. **Target audience**: Our buyer-person would be a high-end, tech-savvy car enthusiast and fan of video games, especially those involving driving simulations. They would be people who value immersive experiences, appreciate innovation and are willing to pay for high-quality experiences.

3. **Channels**: The metaverse platform where the virtual driving experience would be hosted could be a popular gaming platform such as Unity or Unreal Engine. In addition, the experience could be promoted through automotive and gaming influencers on platforms such as Twitch, YouTube, and Reddit, and at eSports and automotive events.

4. **Immersive experience**: Users could drive a virtual Tesla in a variety of environments (cities, mountains, racetracks) and experience Tesla vehicle features and functionalities such as acceleration, Autopilot and performance in different weather and road conditions.

5. **Sources of income**: Tesla could charge a fee for the virtual driving experience. In addition, it could create a line of NFTs that would include models of its cars, accessories and customizations, and even "experience passes" that would allow access to exclusive experiences within the metaverse.

6. **Key metrics**: Number of users trying the experience, number of NFTs sold, number of actual car reservations made after trying the experience, user feedback.

7. **NFT**: In addition to model cars in NFT format, Tesla could offer NFT of accessories and customizations for the cars, allowing users to customize their car in the metaverse. It could also offer "experience passes" in NFT format that would give access to exclusive experiences, such as

driving on iconic race tracks or testing the latest models prior to their launch.

8. **Competitive advantage**: Tesla is a recognized and respected brand in the automotive industry with advanced technology. Your virtual test drive experience would benefit from your reputation and technological competence.

9. **Key alliances**: Metaverse platforms with strong simulation and physics capabilities, virtual reality companies to provide hardware (e.g. VR driving wheels, pedals), eSports companies to organize events and competitions.

10. **Cost structure**: Development and maintenance of the virtual driving experience, partnerships and licensing, marketing and promotion, customer support, regulatory and compliance.

6.3. National Geographic: Virtual Travel and Exploration

National Geographic could use the metaverse to take its audiences on virtual trips to exotic destinations, historical sites or even outer space. This action would not only provide an educational and entertaining user experience, but would also reinforce National Geographic's brand as a leader in global exploration and education. The goal would be to increase public participation and expand its reach to new audiences.

Metaverse Canvas: National Geographic

1. **Solution**: National Geographic could create a unique virtual travel and exploration experience. Through immersive and detailed recreations of iconic sites and nature reserves, learning and appreciation of the planet and its diverse cultures would be promoted.

2. **Target audience**: The main target audience would be travel enthusiasts, educators and students, as well as those interested in history and geography. In addition, this service could also attract those looking for immersive and exciting experiences in the metaverse.

3. **Channels**: The main metaverse platforms would be the main channels for this experience, as well as social networks, where the different experiences and virtual trips could be promoted. They could also be promoted on the National Geographic website and magazine.

4. **Immersive Experience**: The immersive experience would provide an interactive and educational environment, where users could explore the most remote places on the planet, learn about different cultures and the history of the Earth, all in first person.

5. **Sources of Income**: Revenue sources would come primarily from ticket sales for virtual travel experiences. They could also sell NFTs of iconic photographs, videos and digital artifacts related to the different locations and experiences.

6. **Key Metrics**: Key metrics would be the number of tickets sold for the experiences, user engagement time, number of NFTs sold, and interaction on social media and metaverse platforms.

7. **NFTs**: As mentioned, NFTs could be an integral part of the experience, allowing users to purchase and collect iconic photographs, videos and digital artifacts, adding an element of exclusivity and ownership to the experience.

8. **Competitive Advantage**: National Geographic's competitive advantage lies in its wealth of high-quality content, its reputation as a renowned educational and research entity, and its expertise in creating immersive and educational experiences.

9. **Key Alliances**: Key partnerships could be with metaverse platforms, other educational and research organizations, and possibly governments and tourism agencies to help accurately recreate different places and cultures.

10. **Cost Structure**: Costs involved would include developing and maintaining the metaverse platform, creating and updating content, promoting and selling tickets and NFTs, and possibly licensing and partnerships.

6.4. Adidas: Customization and Sale of Virtual Clothing

Adidas could be activated in the metaverse to allow users to customize and purchase virtual branded apparel for their avatars. This action would not only provide a new e-commerce platform for the brand, but would also allow users to express their individuality and brand affiliation in the virtual environment. The objective would be to generate additional sales and reinforce brand loyalty.

Metaverse Canvas: Adidas

1. **Solution**: Adidas could create a virtual apparel customization platform in the metaverse. Users would have the ability to customize and purchase Adidas apparel items for their avatars and characters in the metaverse.

2. **Target Audience**: Metaverse users interested in fashion and in customizing their avatars with well-known brands. This group may include young millennials and generation Z, interested in fashion, technology and virtual worlds.

3. **Channels**: The Adidas platform in the metaverse would be the main channel for this solution. They could also use social media, gaming platforms, and fashion and technology forums to promote their platform and attract their target audience.

4. **Immersive Experience**: Users will be able to customize and dress their avatars with Adidas clothing in a three-dimensional environment. The platform would offer a wide variety of customization options and allow users to experiment with different styles and combinations.

5. **Sources of Income**: The main sources of revenue would be virtual apparel sales and item customizations. They

could also generate revenue by selling limited edition NFTs of their products.

6. **Key Metrics**: Some of the key metrics could include the number of active users, sales of virtual clothing, the number of customizations made, and the number of NFTs sold.

7. **NFT**: Adidas could launch limited editions of virtual apparel as NFTs. This would not only generate additional revenue, but also add an element of exclusivity and collectibility to their products.

8. **Competitive Advantage**: Adidas is a globally recognized brand with a wide range of products. Its entry into the metaverse would reinforce its position as an innovative and cutting-edge brand in the fashion industry.

9. **Key Alliances**: Adidas could form partnerships with popular metaverse platforms, as well as designers and digital artists to create unique and engaging designs for its virtual apparel.

10. **Cost Structure**: The main costs would be associated with the development and maintenance of the personalization platform, the creation and design of the virtual clothing, and the promotion and marketing of the platform and its products.

6.5. L'Oréal: Virtual Makeup Simulator

L'Oréal could use the metaverse to provide users with a virtual makeup simulator. Users would be able to try different products and makeup styles on their avatars, providing an interactive and personalized user experience. The objective of this action would be to promote experimentation with L'Oréal products and generate sales through a new e-commerce channel.

Metaverse Canvas: L'Oréal

1. **Solution**: L'Oréal could offer a virtual makeup simulator in the metaverse, providing users with a unique makeup testing and customization experience. This simulator would allow users to see what L'Oréal products look like in their avatars in real time, taking the uncertainty out of shopping and improving the customer experience. By providing a tool that facilitates experimentation and exploration of the brand's products, L'Oréal would be bringing value to both potential new and existing customers, thus improving brand perception and positioning in the online beauty market.

2. **Target Audience**: Metaverse users interested in beauty and makeup, particularly young and adult women looking to explore and experiment with beauty products in a new and exciting way.

3. **Channels**: L'Oréal's makeup simulation platform in the metaverse would be the main channel. They could also make use of social media, beauty influencers, and online

beauty blogs and magazines to promote their makeup simulator.

4. **Immersive Experience**: Users could experiment with a wide range of makeup products and create unique looks for their avatars. The platform could offer makeup tutorials and tips, as well as options for saving and sharing favorite looks.

5. **Sources of Income**: L'Oréal could monetize the platform through the sale of virtual makeup products for avatars, as well as by selling physical beauty products directly from the platform. NFTs could also be a source of revenue, selling limited edition products or exclusive makeup looks.

6. **Key Metrics**: Key metrics could include the number of active users, the number of makeup products sold (virtual and physical), and user participation in tutorials and other activities on the platform.

7. **NFT**: L'Oréal could sell NFTs of exclusive makeup looks or limited edition products. These NFTs could be collectible or could be used by users' avatars in the metaverse.

8. **Competitive Advantage**: L'Oréal is a leading brand in the beauty industry and has a wide range of high quality products. Its entry into the metaverse with an innovative virtual makeup solution would reinforce its position as an innovative brand in the sector.

9. **Key Alliances**: L'Oréal could team up with popular metaverse platforms and beauty influencers to promote its makeup simulator.

10. **Cost Structure**: The main costs would include the development and maintenance of the makeup simulation platform, the creation of virtual makeup products, and the promotion and marketing of the platform and its products.

6.6. Tours Virtuales - Lonely Planet

Lonely Planet, famous for its travel guides, could leverage the metaverse to offer immersive virtual tours of tourist destinations around the world. Users could explore these places in 3D, learning about their history, culture and tourist attractions in an interactive way. This approach could not only offer a new way to experience tourism, but could also promote sustainable tourism by reducing the need for physical travel.

Metaverse Canvas: Lonely Planet

1. **Solution**: Lonely Planet could offer interactive virtual tours in the metaverse. This service would allow users to explore popular and unknown tourist destinations around the world, learning about the history, culture, cuisine and other local features in an immersive and engaging way.

2. **Target Audience**: Travelers and culture lovers who value the convenience, accessibility and authenticity of online

tourism experiences, especially those familiar with the metaverse and immersive technologies.

3. **Channels**: Popular metaverse platforms such as Decentraland and Cryptovoxels, Lonely Planet social media channels, online travel ticketing and booking platforms, and VR/AR/MR events and conventions.

4. **Immersive Experience**: Users could navigate through first-person virtual tours, interact with objects and points of interest, participate in local activities and events, and socialize with other users and local guides in real time.

5. **Sources of Income**: Users could purchase access tickets to virtual tours, purchase souvenir NFTs and digital collectibles, and book additional services and activities. In addition, Lonely Planet could monetize partnerships and sponsorships with local tourism organizations and businesses.

6. **Key Metrics**: The number of users and tickets sold, the time spent on virtual tours, the level of user interaction and satisfaction, the number and value of NFTs sold, and the impact of partnerships and sponsorships.

7. **NFTs**: Lonely Planet could issue NFTs of digital souvenirs and collectibles that users could purchase, trade and display during and after virtual tours. These NFTs could represent users' unique experiences and achievements, adding value and meaning to their virtual adventures.

8. **Competitive Advantage**: Lonely Planet could leverage its recognized brand, high-quality travel content, network

of local guides and experts, and experience in the travel community to offer authentic and engaging virtual tours that other competitors might struggle to replicate.

9. **Key Alliances**: Lonely Planet could establish partnerships with metaverse platforms, local tourism organizations and businesses, VR/AR/MR technologies and platforms, and online travel creators and communities, to enhance its metaverse offering and performance.

10. **Cost Structure**: Lonely Planet's primary costs would include the development and maintenance of virtual tours, user acquisition and retention, channel management and promotion, production and sale of NFTs, and regulatory and compliance.

6.7. Tour Guide Training - World Tourism Organization

The World Tourism Organization could use the metaverse to provide training and education for tour guides and other tourism professionals. Participants could practice skills in virtual environments that replicate real-world situations, allowing them to learn and improve more effectively. This could also enable the participation of people from all over the world, which would promote inclusion and diversity in the tourism industry.

Metaverse Canvas: World Tourism Organization

1. **Solution**: The World Tourism Organization (UNWTO) could implement a tour guide training program in

the metaverse, providing an immersive and highly interactive environment for training. Guides could learn and practice key skills, such as presentations in various languages, knowledge of tourist sites and customer service, in a variety of simulated scenarios.

2. **Target Audience**: Tour guides and aspiring guides around the world who wish to improve their skills and knowledge, as well as tourism companies looking to train their staff in a more effective and attractive way.

3. **Channels**: Popular metaverse platforms, professional and tourism training portals, tourism industry events and partnerships with national and regional tourism organizations.

4. **Immersive Experience**: Participants could interact with tourist avatars, answer their questions, solve problems and adapt to different situations. They could virtually visit various destinations and learn about their history, culture and attractions.

5. **Sources of Income**: Enrollment in training programs, sale of specialized training material in NFT format, sponsorships and collaborations with tourism companies.

6. **Key Metrics**: Number of program participants, program evaluations, number of certified guides, levels of participation and interaction, and test and evaluation results.

7. **NFTs**: They could create NFTs of training materials, certificates and badges of achievement that participants could collect and share.

8. **Competitive Advantage**: UNWTO could leverage its authority and expertise in the tourism industry, as well as its global network of partnerships, to deliver a high-caliber training program that would be difficult to replicate.

9. **Key Alliances**: Partnerships with national and regional tourism organizations, tourism and hospitality companies, training and staff development experts, and metaverse technology companies.

10. **Cost Structure**: The main costs would be related to the development and maintenance of the metaverse training program, content creation, participant acquisition and retention, and regulatory compliance.

6.8. Virtual Catwalks - Gucci

Gucci, known for its bold approach to fashion, could tap into the metaverse to take its famous runways to a new level. They could create a virtual space where users could attend fashion shows in real time, with 3D models showing off the brand's latest collections. In addition, users could interact with the garments, exploring their details up close and even try them on their avatars. This would not only provide an immersive and interactive experience, but would also allow Gucci to reach a global audience in a more direct and personal way. This strategy would also be a great complement to its Gucci Virtual 25 line, a pair of sneakers designed exclusively for the virtual world.

Metaverse Canvas: Gucci

1. **Solution**: Gucci could innovate in the metaverse space by implementing virtual catwalks. Users could attend fashion shows in real time, view new collections and purchase limited edition virtual clothing pieces for their avatars.

2. **Target Audience**: Fashion lovers, influencers, high-end shoppers and regular Gucci customers who are interested in virtual fashion and exclusive experiences.

3. **Channels**: Popular metaverse platforms such as Decentraland or Crypto Voxels, Gucci's social media channels, email newsletters and Gucci's own website.

4. **Immersive Experience**: Users could attend 3D fashion shows, interact with other attendees, explore new collections in a virtual environment and purchase exclusive virtual Gucci apparel for their avatars.

5. **Sources of Income**: Sale of virtual clothing NFTs, tickets to exclusive fashion shows, collaborations with influencers and cross-selling of physical products through Gucci's online store.

6. **Key Metrics**: Parade attendees, NFTs sold, user interactions and engagement, media coverage, new social media followers and cross-selling.

7. **NFTs**: Gucci could launch virtual wearables as NFTs. Buyers could use these pieces in their avatars, and NFTs could increase in value based on their rarity and demand.

8. **Competitive Advantage**: As one of the world's most recognized luxury fashion brands, Gucci has a considerable competitive advantage. The brand can use its reputation and existing relationships with designers, influencers and celebrities to attract a wide audience to its virtual catwalks.

9. **Key Alliances**: Metaverse platforms, fashion designers, fashion influencers and celebrities, and NFT platforms.

10. **Cost Structure**: The costs of virtual runway development and maintenance, virtual fashion design, event management and promotion, and regulatory and compliance.

6.9. Immersive Match Experience - LaLiga

LaLiga, the leading professional soccer league in Spain, could create a soccer metaverse where fans around the world could have an immersive match experience. In this virtual space, fans could not only watch matches in real time with a 360-degree perspective, but also interact with other fans, visit virtual stadiums and participate in soccer-related games and activities.

In addition, they could offer exclusive content, such as live interviews with players and coaches, locker room tours and training sessions, and provide fans with a unique experience they can't get through traditional TV or internet channels.

Creating this immersive experience in the metaverse would also open up new sponsorship and monetization opportunities for LaLiga. For example, virtual match tickets, digital merchandising products and virtual stadium naming rights could be sold. This would allow LaLiga to generate additional revenue and attract a wider global audience.

Metaverse Canvas: La Liga

1. **Solution**: LaLiga could take advantage of the potential of the metaverse to offer immersive experiences in soccer matches. Users could "attend" their favorite teams' games in real time from the point of view of a spectator in the stadium, interact with other fans and collect exclusive match-related items such as NFTs of highlights.

2. **Target Audience**: Soccer fans, LaLiga followers, collectors of sports NFTs and gamers looking for new ways to interact with their favorite teams.

3. **Channels**: Metaverse platforms such as Decentraland, LaLiga social networks, email newsletters and LaLiga's own website.

4. **Immersive Experience**: Users could experience the excitement of soccer matches as if they were in the stadium, interact with other fans, collect NFTs of memorable moments and participate in exclusive virtual events.

5. **Sources of Income**: Sale of match-related NFTs, virtual tickets for exclusive experiences, sponsorships and partnerships, and cross-selling of physical LaLiga products.

6. **Key Metrics**: Virtual attendance at games, NFTs sold, user interactions, media coverage, new followers on social networks and cross-selling.

7. **NFTs**: LaLiga could release NFTs of memorable match moments, virtual tickets for exclusive experiences and other match-related collectibles.

8. **Competitive Advantage**: As one of the most popular and prestigious soccer leagues in the world, LaLiga has a significant competitive advantage. It could use its reputation, large fan base and relationships with clubs and players to attract a large audience to its metaverse experiences.

9. **Key Alliances**: Metaverse platforms, LaLiga soccer clubs, players, sponsors and NFT platforms.

10. **Cost Structure**: The costs of developing and maintaining the immersive experience, producing NFTs, managing and promoting virtual games, and complying with regulations and standards.

6.10. Virtual Campus in Metaverso - Business School

A business school could expand its physical boundaries by creating a virtual campus in the metaverse. This digital infrastructure would provide an interactive and immersive environment for teaching and learning, remove geographical barriers and allow students from all over the world to access the high quality education offered by the school.

In this virtual campus, students could attend lectures and seminars in real time, participate in group discussions and debates, and work on team projects. They could also interact with teachers and classmates, visit the virtual library and use digital learning resources.

In addition, the business school could host virtual job fairs and networking events, and would allow students to connect with recruiters and industry professionals. Business case competitions and hackathons could also be organized, and allow students to present their ideas and projects to investors and entrepreneurs.

This presence in the metaverse could also be a source of revenue for the business school, through the sale of online courses and training programs, consulting and coaching services, and digital certificates and diplomas.

Metaverse Canvas: Business School

1. **Solution**: The business school could develop a virtual campus in the metaverse that would offer an immersive educational experience. Students could attend classes in real time, interact with professors and classmates, participate in networking activities and access exclusive learning resources.

2. **Target Audience**: Current and prospective business students, professionals looking to improve their skills, and people interested in online education and the metaverse.

3. **Channels**: Metaverse platforms such as Decentraland or Spatial, the business school's social networks and website, and online education platforms.

4. **Immersive Experience**: Users could attend virtual classes, interact with other students and teachers, participate in networking events and access educational resources in an interactive virtual environment.

5. **Sources of Income**: Course tuition, advertising and sponsorships, sale of exclusive learning resources, and paid networking events.

6. **Key Metrics**: Number of students enrolled, level of participation in classes and events, student satisfaction, and conversions from prospects to enrolled students.

7. **NFTs**: The business school may issue NFTs that represent diplomas or certificates of course completion, achievement badges and unique learning resources.

8. **Competitive Advantage**: As an established business school, it has a reputation and experience in offering high quality business programs. Its virtual campus in the metaverse allows it to stand out in the increasingly competitive online education market.

9. **Key Alliances**: Metaverse platforms, partner educational institutions, companies offering internship

or employment opportunities to students, and online education platforms.

10. **Cost Structure**: Development and maintenance of the virtual campus, hiring of teachers and support staff, creation of educational content, and compliance with educational regulations and standards.

6.11. BBVA: Immersive Virtual Banking

BBVA could launch a virtual banking experience in the metaverse to take its financial services to a new level. This proposal would involve the creation of a virtual BBVA branch in the metaverse, where users could access their bank accounts, perform transactions and get advice from customer service agents in real time and in an immersive way.

In this virtual environment, customers could explore different banking products and services, receive personalized financial advice and interact with other users. This project would expand BBVA's digital presence, improve customer interaction and could attract a new segment of customers interested in immersive technologies.

Metaverse Canvas: BBVA

1. **Solution**: Virtual BBVA branch in the metaverse, offering an immersive real-time banking experience. Customers could conduct transactions, receive advice and explore banking products and services.

2. **Target audience**: Current and potential BBVA customers interested in metaverse technology and improving their banking experience. This group could include young professionals, entrepreneurs and technology enthusiasts.

3. **Channels**: BBVA's virtual branch on various metaverse platforms such as Decentraland, Somnium Space, etc., its official website and mobile banking applications.

4. **Immersive experience**: Users would be able to interact with BBVA's virtual branch interface as if they were in a physical branch, conduct banking transactions, attend financial webinars and receive personalized advice from BBVA's artificial intelligence agents.

5. **Sources of income**: Revenues would come from commissions from transactions conducted through the metaverse platform, the sale of financial products and services, and possible partnerships with other entities or companies in the metaverse.

6. **Key metrics**: Number of active users, transactions made on the metaverse platform, participation in webinars or virtual events, and customer satisfaction.

7. **NFT**: Ability to offer tokenized financial products such as NFT, and allow customers to trade these assets within the platform.

8. **Competitive advantage**: BBVA would become one of the first banks to offer an immersive banking experience in the metaverse, strengthening its brand image as an innovator in digital financial services.

9. **Key alliances**: Potential partnerships with metaverse platforms, blockchain technology providers, and other companies looking to explore the financial services space in the metaverse.

10. **Cost structure**: Initial investment in the development and deployment of the virtual branch, platform maintenance, regulatory compliance and costs associated with alliances and agreements with metaverse platforms.

7

FUTURE TRENDS AND OPPORTUNITIES IN THE METAVERSE

The metaverse, with its immersive, interactive and highly participatory nature, is revolutionizing the way companies interact with their customers and conduct their business operations. This dynamic and exciting digital reality is driven by continuous technological innovations, which are opening up new ways of doing business and reaching consumers in previously unthinkable ways.

This chapter will therefore provide an in-depth look at the main trends that are shaping the metaverse and how these can be leveraged to open up new business opportunities. From technological innovations and changes in consumer behavior, to the emergence of new possibilities for partnerships and collaborations, this chapter will help readers navigate the cutting edge of this exciting new frontier.

In addition, we will understand how metaverse trends are redefining the concept of customer engagement, enabling companies to create deeper and more meaningful connections with their audiences. In doing so, they are discovering new ways to create value and differentiation in an increasingly competitive marketplace.

In this regard, this chapter will serve as a compass, and provide the keys to navigating the complex but exciting landscape of the metaverse. The future is already here, and it is time to understand it, embrace it and, above all, take advantage of it.

7.1. Technological innovations and their impact on businesses

In the fast-paced world of technology, emerging advances are constantly changing the landscape of the metaverse, offering new opportunities and challenges for businesses. Below we address some of the most significant technological innovations and discuss how they may impact business models in the metaverse.

- **Virtual Reality (VR) and Augmented Reality (AR)**: The continued advancement of VR and AR is changing the way we interact with the metaverse. With more affordable and high-quality devices, these technologies are making the metaverse a more immersive and realistic experience. This opens up new opportunities for companies looking to offer unique experiences to their customers, whether through virtual tours, product trials in AR or immersive gaming experiences in VR.

- **Artificial Intelligence (AI)**: AI has the potential to revolutionize many aspects of the metaverse. From intelligent virtual assistants to personalization algorithms, AI can help companies provide more personalized and efficient experiences to their customers in the metaverse.

- **Blockchain and NFTs**: Blockchain technology and NFTs have proven to be of great importance in the metaverse, enabling digital ownership and monetization of virtual assets. Companies can use these technologies to create new revenue models, such as selling unique digital goods or creating virtual economies.

- **5G and beyond**: The implementation of 5G networks and future network technologies will enable faster and more stable connectivity, which is crucial for a seamless metaverse experience. This could enable richer, real-time experiences in the metaverse, such as live virtual concerts or sporting events.

Each of these technological innovations presents exciting opportunities, but also challenges that must be considered. For example, as VR and AR become more realistic, privacy and security issues become more critical. Similarly, while blockchain and NFTs offer new ways to monetize the metaverse, they also present sustainability and accessibility issues.

As an entrepreneur or marketer in the metaverse, it is vital to stay on top of these innovations and understand how they can affect your business model. Through experimentation and adaptation, you can leverage these technologies to drive growth and success in the metaverse.

7.2. Changes in consumer behavior and target audiences

In the dynamic ecosystem of the metaverse, understanding consumer behavior is an essential component for the creation and evolution of a successful business model. With technological innovations and variations in societal trends, consumer behavior patterns are constantly changing and evolving.

- **Increased demand for immersive experiences**: With the popularization of virtual reality and augmented reality, consumers are increasingly looking for immersive experiences. First-person experiences and interactivity have become key elements that users seek in the metaverse, whether through games, shopping or exploring new virtual worlds.

- **Digital property and virtual economies**: The advent of blockchain technology and NFTs has led to a change in the perception of digital property. Users no longer just consume content, but also seek to own and trade digital goods in virtual economies. This opens up new opportunities for businesses in terms of monetization and value creation.

- **Socialization in the metaverse**: Metaverses are not only platforms for content consumption, but have also become social spaces. Users seek to interact with others, create communities and share experiences. This shift toward socialization in the metaverse offers companies new ways to interact and connect with their audiences.

- **New ways of working and learning**: With the rise of teleworking and e-learning, metaverses are being considered as a new platform for these activities. Companies that can provide efficient and attractive solutions for working and learning in the metaverse will have a great opportunity to grow.

It is essential that companies understand these changes and adapt their strategies and offerings accordingly. The ability to anticipate and respond to consumer behavior trends can be a key determinant of success in the metaverse. At the same time, companies must be aware of the challenges these changes may present, such as the need to protect user privacy and ensure a safe and positive experience in the metaverse.

7.3. New business opportunities and alliances in the metaverse

The metaverse is a constant source of new business opportunities and partnership possibilities. In this expanding digital space, companies can explore a multitude of ways to innovate, grow and collaborate.

- **Creation and trade of digital goods**: The NFT economy has opened new doors for the creation and trade of digital goods. Artists, content creators and businesses can leverage this trend to generate revenue and build communities around their products.

- **Immersive experiences and advertising**: As consumers seek more immersive experiences, companies can explore opportunities in the creation of interactive content, games and virtual reality experiences. In addition, advertising in the metaverse provides a new way to reach consumers in a more engaging and personalized way.

- **Virtual services**: From consulting and education to healthcare and financial services, there is a growing demand for services in the metaverse. Companies that can provide these services efficiently and attractively in the metaverse will have a competitive advantage.

- **Strategic alliances**: Given the collaborative and connected nature of the metaverse, strategic alliances can be a powerful avenue for growth. Companies can collaborate to deliver richer experiences, reach new markets and share resources and knowledge.

- **Innovation in the** workplace: The metaverse also offers new ways of working. Companies can create virtual offices, conduct virtual reality meetings and leverage online collaboration tools to improve productivity and employee satisfaction.

- **Sustainability and social responsibility**: The metaverse also presents an opportunity for companies to demonstrate their commitment to sustainability and social responsibility. Creating virtual experiences that promote environmental awareness, inclusion and diversity can strengthen brand image and attract conscious consumers.

It is crucial, however, to keep in mind that success in the metaverse requires much more than simply moving existing business practices to a new medium. It requires a deep understanding of the digital environment, a willingness to innovate and the ability to adapt quickly to changing consumer trends and expectations.

8

CONCLUSIONS

We have come a long way in this work, unraveling the promising and complex reality of the metaverse, an ever-expanding digital parallel reality that is transforming the way we interact, work, play and do business. From the introduction and definition of the metaverse, to the exploration of the opportunities and challenges that this new digital space implies, we have unpacked each of the components that make it up.

Along the way, the Metaverse Canvas has proven to be an essential tool. As an adaptation of the Business Model Canvas, this framework allows us to analyze in detail and efficiently every facet of a business model in the metaverse, from identifying the solution and target audience, defining channels and the immersive experience, to implementing NFTs and forging key partnerships, among other aspects.

At the same time, we have emphasized the need for continuous adaptation and innovation in this digital environment, as trends change rapidly and emerging technologies, such as NFTs and virtual reality, are redefining the rules of the game.

We have also reviewed success stories and practical applications of the Metaverse Canvas, which has allowed us to emphasize the relevance of this model in the creation and development of successful business strategies in the metaverse.

Finally, we have outlined a glimpse into the future, identifying emerging trends and business opportunities that could make their way into the metaverse, as well as the challenges that this new horizon presents.

8.1. The importance of adaptation and innovation in the metaverse

Adaptation and innovation are two crucial elements for any company or entrepreneur aspiring to succeed in the metaverse. This digital environment is in a constant state of change and evolution, driven by technological advances and changes in consumer behavior patterns.

Adaptation refers to a company's ability to adjust its operations and strategies in response to these changes. In the metaverse, this can involve everything from the adoption of new technologies, such as virtual reality and NFTs, to altering business models to meet changing consumer expectations in terms of immersion and interactivity. Those companies that are able to adapt quickly to new circumstances will have a competitive advantage in this dynamic environment.

On the other hand, innovation is the engine that drives the creation of new solutions and opportunities in the metaverse.

As technologies advance and the possibilities of the metaverse expand, companies have the opportunity to innovate in terms of products, services, experiences and business models. Innovation in the metaverse can take multiple forms, from creating unique immersive experiences to exploring new forms of monetization through NFTs.

8.1.1. Understanding adaptability in the metaverse

The metaverse, as an emerging concept, is constantly evolving and growing. The technology on which it is based changes and updates at a dizzying pace, and user expectations and the possibilities for interaction and participation are continually expanding and transforming. In this context, adaptability becomes an essential competency for any business wishing to operate successfully in the metaverse.

But what does it really mean to be adaptable in the metaverse? Broadly speaking, adaptability in this environment implies an organization's ability to adjust quickly to changes in technology, market trends and user preferences. It means being able to identify and respond to new opportunities and challenges as they arise, and to evolve and transform one's operations, products or services in response to these changing circumstances.

Adaptability in the metaverse also implies a level of flexibility and resilience in the face of uncertainty and risk. Because the metaverse is relatively uncharted territory, with rules and dynamics that are still being defined, organizations must be prepared to deal with unexpected and sometimes difficult situations. This requires an open mind and a willingness to learn, to experiment and to accept failure as part of the innovation process.

Finally, adaptability in the metaverse entails a willingness to collaborate and co-create with others. In such a vast and diverse environment, where the boundaries between different worlds and experiences are fluid, organizations that are able to establish partnerships and work together with others will be better able to take advantage of opportunities and deal more effectively with challenges.

8.1.2. Adaptability case studies

Here are some case studies that illustrate how different organizations have demonstrated adaptability in the metaverse.

1. **Epic Games and Fortnite**: Epic Games, the company behind Fortnite, has demonstrated remarkable adaptability in the metaverse. At first, Fortnite was simply a shooter video game, but Epic Games has transformed it into a social entertainment platform with live events, collaborations with brands and artists, and a robust virtual economy. This adaptation to new opportunities and trends has contributed to Fortnite's huge success.

2. **Roblox Corporation**: Roblox is another platform that has demonstrated a great capacity for adaptation. While initially focused on providing a space for children to

play and create games, the platform has expanded to include virtual learning experiences, live events and collaborations with brands. Roblox has demonstrated remarkable flexibility in adapting to the changing expectations and needs of its growing user base.

3. **LVMH and League of Legends**: LVMH, the luxury brand conglomerate, has demonstrated adaptability in its approach to the metaverse through its collaboration with League of Legends, a popular online video game. LVMH designed and created virtual outfits for the game's characters, adapting to the growing fashion trend in the metaverse and reaching a new audience.

These case studies highlight how adaptability in the metaverse can take many forms and how it can be a significant strategic advantage. Organizations that are able to adapt quickly and effectively to the changing circumstances of the metaverse will be better positioned to succeed in this emerging environment.

8.1.3. Understanding innovation in the metaverse

Innovation in the metaverse is a multifaceted and powerful concept that plays a critical role in shaping this new digital world. In simple terms, innovation can be defined as the implementation of new ideas, concepts, products or processes to significantly improve the effectiveness or efficiency of an organization. However, in the context of the metaverse, innovation takes on an additional dimension.

First, innovation in the metaverse can involve the creation of unique and immersive immersive experiences. Companies can innovate by designing virtual spaces that offer users new ways to interact and participate. For example, live virtual concerts, digital art exhibitions and virtual learning experiences are all forms of innovation in the metaverse.

In addition, innovation in the metaverse may be related to the underlying technology and infrastructure. This includes the development of technologies such as blockchain, artificial intelligence, virtual and augmented reality, and other emerging technologies that are fundamental to the existence and functioning of the metaverse.

Finally, innovation in the metaverse can also refer to the creation of new forms of governance, economy and ownership. NFTs, for example, have innovated the way digital assets are owned and traded, while DAOs (Decentralized Autonomous Organizations) are redefining forms of governance in the metaverse.

It is crucial to understand that innovation in the metaverse is a continuous process. Companies that want to succeed in this new environment must be willing to constantly adapt and evolve, explore new ideas and embrace emerging technologies. Innovation in the metaverse is not an end goal, but an ongoing journey of discovery, experimentation and learning.

8.1.4. Innovation case studies

In this section, we will examine some outstanding case studies that illustrate how innovation can drive success in the metaverse.

1. **Epic Games and Fortnite**: Epic Games has innovated on multiple fronts with Fortnite, transforming a simple battle game into a vibrant and constantly evolving metaverse. It has introduced innovative concepts such as virtual concerts, where artists such as Travis Scott have performed in virtual concerts that have attracted millions of viewers. In addition, Epic Games is innovating in building the metaverse infrastructure through its Unreal Engine, which is driving the creation of digital worlds in numerous industries.

2. **Decentraland and virtual property**: Decentraland is a virtual universe where users can own and develop parcels of virtual land, represented as NFTs on the Ethereum blockchain. This innovative approach to virtual land ownership and development has enabled users to create everything from virtual casinos to digital art galleries.

3. **Roblox and the creator economy**: Roblox is another metaverse platform that has innovated by allowing users to create and sell their own games and experiences within the platform. This creator economy has resulted in a thriving ecosystem where users can earn real money through their digital creations.

4. **Facebook/Meta and the metaverse vision**: Facebook, now known as Meta, is innovating in building an interconnected metaverse. With its vision of "Horizon Workrooms", Meta is working on creating collaborative virtual workspaces and integrating different platforms and services into a unified metaverse.

These case studies show how innovation can take many forms in the metaverse. Whether through creating unique immersive experiences, developing new forms of ownership and economics, or building the underlying infrastructure of the metaverse, innovation is the key to navigating and thriving in this new digital world.

8.1.5. How to foster adaptability and innovation

Adaptability and innovation are two fundamental skills that any business must cultivate to succeed in the metaverse. Below are some strategies for fostering these skills:

1. **Constant learning mentality**: The metaverse is constantly evolving, which requires a constant learning mentality. Companies must be willing to explore new trends, adopt new technologies and adapt to changing user expectations. This may involve investing in ongoing training for the team, as well as creating an organizational culture that values and rewards curiosity and experimentation.

2. **Experimentation and risk taking**: Innovation often involves risk-taking and experimentation. Companies

must be willing to try new ideas, even if some of them fail. It is essential to establish a safe space for experimentation, where failures are seen as learning opportunities.

3. **Collaboration and partnership**: The metaverse is a highly interconnected space, offering ample opportunities for collaboration and partnership. Companies can foster innovation by working with other companies, content creators, and the user community. Partnerships can enable access to new skills, technologies and audiences.

4. **Focus on the user**: Adaptability and innovation must always be oriented towards creating value for the user. This implies a deep understanding of user needs and expectations and a willingness to adapt and evolve the company's offerings based on these insights. User data collection and analysis can be valuable tools to guide this user-centered adaptation and innovation.

5. **Investment in technology and development**: To innovate in the metaverse, it is essential to invest in technology and development. This may involve the adoption of emerging technologies such as virtual and augmented reality, artificial intelligence, or blockchain. It may also involve investment in software and hardware development, as well as IT infrastructure.

Fostering adaptability and innovation is not an easy task, but it is essential for success in the metaverse. By cultivating a constant learning mindset, encouraging experimentation and risk-taking, collaborating and partnering with others, focusing on the user, and investing in technology and development, companies can position themselves at the forefront of this new digital world.

8.2. Metaverse Canvas as a key tool for success in the metaverse

The Metaverse Canvas is a framework that helps companies understand and design their business model in the metaverse, an emerging virtual environment with enormous growth potential. This tool enables organizations to clearly identify their value proposition, the customer segments they are targeting, the channels through which they can reach those customers, the relationships they need to establish with them, the key activities they need to perform, the resources they need, their key partners, their cost structure and their revenue streams.

The use of the Metaverse Canvas can provide a number of advantages for companies wishing to operate in the metaverse. First, it enables organizations to clearly and concisely visualize their business model, which can facilitate both strategic decision making and communication of the business model to stakeholders.

Second, it can help companies identify and focus on the most important aspects of their business model, which can lead to greater efficiency and effectiveness. Third, it can provide companies with a roadmap for the creation, development and consolidation of their presence in the metaverse.

However, for the Metaverse Canvas to be truly effective, it is crucial that companies use it in the right way. This involves correctly understanding the different components of the Metaverse Canvas, knowing how they interrelate with each other and being able to apply this knowledge to the concrete reality of your business. In addition, it is essential that companies are willing to adapt and revise their Metaverse Canvas as both their business and the metaverse itself evolve.

8.3. The future of business in the metaverse: prospects and challenges.

The metaverse, like any new paradigm, presents a future full of possibilities and challenges. This new emerging digital universe represents a unique opportunity for companies to redefine their business models, interact with consumers in innovative ways and open up new avenues for growth. However, it also poses significant challenges, from technical issues to legal and ethical issues.

8.3.1. Technological advances and their influence on the metaverse

Technological advances are one of the key drivers behind the evolution and growth of the metaverse. The speed with which these developments are occurring means that the metaverse is constantly changing, presenting new opportunities and challenges for companies.

First, the development of virtual reality (VR) and augmented reality (AR) technologies is transforming the way we interact with the metaverse. Advances in these technologies are enabling more immersive experiences, which in turn is opening up new opportunities for companies to interact with their customers in innovative ways. At the same time, growing consumer adoption of these technologies is driving demand for quality content and experiences in the metaverse.

Second, increasing computing power and improvements in the speed and capacity of telecommunications networks (such as 5G technology) make the metaverse more accessible and appealing to a wider audience. This is enabling companies to reach a global audience in a way that was not possible before.

Third, advances in blockchain technology enable new forms of ownership and transaction in the metaverse. Non-fungible tokens (NFTs) are enabling digital ownership of assets in the metaverse, opening up new opportunities for companies in terms of monetization and customer engagement.

Last but not least, advances in artificial intelligence (AI) and machine learning are enabling more personalized and adaptive experiences in the metaverse, which in turn is enabling companies to give customers what they want, when they want it.

However, these technological advances also pose challenges. Privacy and security issues, the digital divide and ethical issues are just some of the challenges that companies must consider when navigating the metaverse. Despite these challenges, technological advances represent a great opportunity for companies willing to adapt and evolve in this exciting new digital universe.

8.3.2. Changes in consumer behavior

The emergence of the metaverse is redefining how consumers interact, communicate and consume. These changes in consumer behavior are creating both challenges and opportunities for companies.

First, consumers are increasingly familiar with digital technologies and expect experiences that are immersive and interactive. This means that companies must provide experiences in the metaverse that are engaging, personalized and deliver real value. Consumers are no longer mere spectators, but active participants who want to co-create and contribute to the experience.

Second, consumers increasingly value authenticity and transparency, and expect companies to operate in an ethical and responsible manner. This means that companies must be transparent in their business practices and demonstrate a genuine commitment to social and environmental responsibility in the metaverse.

Third, consumers are increasingly looking for experiences that allow them to connect and socialize with others. Companies, therefore, should look for ways to foster these connections and build communities around their brands in the metaverse.

Finally, the emergence of the token economy and NFTs is changing the way consumers own and value digital goods. This represents a new opportunity for companies to monetize their offerings and build new forms of customer engagement.

However, these changes in consumer behavior also pose challenges. Companies must be able to keep up with the rapid and constant evolutions in consumer expectations and behaviors, and must be prepared to adapt and evolve along with them. Those companies that are able to do so will be in an ideal position to succeed in the metaverse.

8.3.3. New business opportunities

The metaverse is giving rise to an entirely new and exciting business ecosystem. As the metaverse continues to evolve, business opportunities are expanding in several directions and new ways to generate revenue are being created.

One of the main drivers of these new business opportunities is the token economy and NFTs. These enable the creation of new business models based on digital ownership, the monetization of virtual assets and the creation of new forms of customer engagement and interaction.

In addition, the growing demand for immersive and interactive experiences is giving rise to new opportunities in the creation of content and services in the metaverse. This includes the design and development of virtual spaces, the creation of virtual and augmented reality experiences, and the provision of online services that enhance the user experience in the metaverse.

On the other hand, the interconnectivity of the metaverse facilitates the creation of new forms of collaboration and cooperation between companies. This is opening up opportunities for the creation of strategic alliances and the formation of business ecosystems, in which companies can work together to offer added value to users.

Finally, the growing importance of social and environmental responsibility in the metaverse is giving rise to new business opportunities in the field of sustainability. This includes creating solutions that minimize the environmental impact of metaverse technologies and providing services that promote equity and inclusion in the metaverse.

However, companies must be aware that the metaverse also presents challenges and risks, and that they must address these challenges responsibly and ethically in order to succeed in this new business environment.

8.3.4. Future challenges and risks

In parallel to the emerging opportunities, the metaverse also presents a series of challenges and risks that companies will have to face and manage in order to ensure their success and sustainability in this new business environment.

One of the most notable challenges lies in the area of data security and privacy. As users interact in the metaverse, they generate a large amount of data that must be properly managed and protected. Companies should ensure that they comply with data privacy laws and regulations and implement robust security measures to protect user data.

Another important challenge is related to interoperability and standardization. Since the metaverse is a conglomerate of different virtual worlds and platforms, ensuring compatibility and interoperability between these environments can be a complex task. Companies will need to collaborate with other organizations and standards developers to ensure that users can move and interact freely between different environments in the metaverse.

Sustainability is another significant challenge. As the metaverse grows and develops, its environmental impact could increase significantly, due to the energy consumption of virtual and augmented reality technologies, and the mining and trading of cryptocurrencies and NFTs. Companies should strive to minimize this impact and promote sustainable practices in the metaverse.

Finally, there is the challenge of equity and inclusion. It is essential to ensure that all people, regardless of location, economic capacity, race, gender or disability, have the opportunity to access and participate in the metaverse. Companies should work to remove barriers to access and promote diversity and inclusion in their activities in the metaverse.

These challenges and risks should not be viewed as insurmountable barriers, but rather as critical areas of focus, which companies should proactively and ethically address on their journey into the metaverse.

9

APPENDIX

9.1. Metaverse Canvas template for practical use

A digital version of the Metaverse Canvas is available for download at https://www.metaversecanvas.org.

9.2. Glossary of terms related to the metaverse and digital marketing

- **5G**: Fifth generation mobile communications technology, which offers faster data rates, higher network capacity and lower latency than previous generations.

- **AI(Artificial Intelligence)**: Technology that mimics human intelligence to perform complex tasks, from speech and image recognition to decision making.

- **Avatar**: In the context of the metaverse, an avatar is the digital representation of a user. It can be as simple as a user name or as complex as a customizable three-dimensional figure.

- **Big Data**: Extremely large set of data that can be computationally analyzed to reveal patterns, trends and associations, especially related to human behavior and interactions.

- **Blockchain**: Distributed registration technology that allows parties to transact securely, without the need for a central intermediary. It is fundamental to cryptocurrencies and smart contract technology.

- **Buyer Persona**: A detailed, semi-fictional profile of an ideal customer based on market and real customer data, which helps companies understand and meet their customers' needs.

- **Smart Contracts**: Computer programs that automatically run on the blockchain when certain predetermined conditions are met.

- **Cryptocurrency**: A type of digital currency based on blockchain technology, which is used as a medium of exchange in digital transactions. Bitcoin and Ether are examples of cryptocurrencies.

- **DAO (Decentralized Autonomous Organization)**: It is an organization represented by rules encoded in a computer program that is transparent, controlled by token holders and not influenced by a central authority.

- **Token economy**: Economic model that uses digital tokens (usually on the blockchain) as a medium of exchange to incentivize or facilitate certain behaviors or actions in a system.

- **Digital Ecosystem**: Set of technologies, applications, people and companies that interact to facilitate and carry out transactions and processes through digital media.

- **Engagement**: The interaction or engagement of users with a product, service or brand in digital media, which can be measured through various actions, such as clicks, "likes", shares, comments, etc.

- **Immersive experience**: Refers to the technology and design of experiences that simulate a physical environment through digital media, creating a sense of presence and participation in that environment.

- **Gamification**: Practice applying game design elements and principles to non-game contexts to enhance user engagement, motivation and user experience.

- **Immersion**: In the metaverse and in virtual reality experiences, immersion refers to the feeling of being fully present and engaged in a digital environment, to the point of forgetting that it is virtual.

- **Interface**: It is the means by which the user interacts with a system or software. It can be graphical (GUI), command line (CLI) or voice-based.

- **Internet of Things (IoT)**: A network of interconnected physical devices that collect and share data over the Internet.

- **Interoperability**: The ability of different computer systems or software to communicate and share information with each other, regardless of manufacturer, platform or operating system.

- **IoT (Internet of Things)**: It is a network of physical objects, vehicles, buildings and others that have sensors and software to collect and share data.

- **Content Marketing**: A marketing strategy that focuses on the creation and distribution of relevant, valuable and consistent content to attract and retain a clearly defined audience, with the goal of driving customer action.

- **Marketing Digital**: Practices of promoting products or brands through digital media, including social networks, search engines, email, and other online communication channels.

- **Metaverse Marketing**: Marketing practices that take place in the metaverse. They include strategies for brand building, customer engagement, and monetization in immersive digital environments.

- **Metaverse**: A persistent and interconnected digital universe that includes multiple virtual realities, where users can interact in real time with the environment, other users and objects.

- **Persistent world**: In the context of video games and metaverses, a persistent world is a virtual world that continues to exist and change even when users are not present.

- **Virtual World**: A simulated online environment in which users can interact with each other and with the environment.

- **NFT (Non Fungible Token)**: A type of digital token on the blockchain that represents a unique asset, and can be owned and traded. NFTs can represent a variety of unique assets, both tangible and intangible.

- **Nube Computacional (Cloud Computing)**: Delivery of IT services over the Internet, allowing users to access applications and data from any Internet-connected device.

- **Augmented Reality (AR)**: Technology that superimposes digital information, such as images and sounds, over the real world, creating a composite experience that can be interacted with in real time.

- **Extended Reality (XR)**: General term that includes all virtual reality (VR), augmented reality (AR), and mixed reality (MR) technologies. The XR combines real-world and digital elements to create an immersive experience.

- **Mixed Reality (MR)**: Technology that merges the real and virtual worlds to produce new environments and visualizations in which physical and digital objects coexist and can interact in real time.

- **Virtual Reality (VR)**: A computer-generated three-dimensional environment that can be explored and interacted with by an individual, creating a sense of physical presence in that environment.

- **SaaS (Software as a Service)**: A software business model in which a vendor hosts and maintains an application on its own servers, and customers access it over the Internet, usually on a subscription basis.

- **SEM (Search Engine Marketing)**: Marketing strategy that seeks to increase the visibility of a website in search engine results, mainly through pay-per-click advertising.

- **SEO (Search Engine Optimization)**: The process of optimizing a website to appear in search engine search results, increasing visibility and organic traffic.

- **Distributed System**: It is a system whose components are located in different network nodes that communicate and coordinate to achieve a common goal.

- **Tokenization of assets:** The process of converting ownership rights of a physical or intangible asset into a digital token on a blockchain.

- **UX (User Experience)**: Design practice that is concerned with how a user feels when interacting with a system, seeking to provide positive experiences to increase user satisfaction and loyalty.

- **Web 3.0**: Also known as the semantic web, it refers to a future generation of the Internet that is smarter, more personalized and more machine-understandable. In Web 3.0, machines will be able to read and interpret the Web in the same way as humans.

www.ingramcontent.com/pod-product-compliance
Lightning Source LLC
LaVergne TN
LVHW051322050326
832903LV00031B/3311